The Career Guide for Creative and Unconventional People

The **C**areer **G**uide for **C**reative and **U**nconventional **P**eople

Carol Eikleberry, Ph.D.

Introduction by
Richard Nelson Bolles

✌ TEN SPEED PRESS
Berkeley, California

Ten Speed Press
Box 7123
Berkeley, California 94707

Design by Catherine Jacobes

Table on pages 6-7 and first drawing on page 10 reproduced by special permission of the Publisher, Psychological Assesment Resources, Inc., from *Making Vocational Choices,* copyright 1973, 1985, and 1992 by Psychological Assesment Resources, Inc. All rights reserved.

Second drawing on page 10 adapted from *Coming Alive from Nine to Five: The Career Search Handbook,* 2nd ed. © 1984 by Betty Neville Michelozzi. Used by permission of the publisher, Mayfield Publishing Co.

Library of Congress Cataloging-in-Publication Data

Eikleberry, Carol.
Career guide for creative and unconventional people / Carol Eikleberry.
    p.   cm.
Includes bibliographical references.
ISBN 0-89815-757-9
    1. Vocational guidance.   2. Creative ability.   I. Title.
HF5381.E485   1995
331.7'02--dc20   95-9018
                                                                      CIP

HF 5381
.E 485
Printed in Canada   *1995*

First printing, 1995

1 2 3 4 5 6 7 8 9 10 — 99 98 97 96 95

Distributed in Australia by E. J. Dwyer Pty. Ltd., in Canada by Publishers Group West, in New Zealand by Tandem Press, in South Africa by Real Books, and in the United Kingdom and Europe by Airlift Books.

Contents

~~~~~~

Acknowledgements. vii

Introduction by Richard Nelson Bolles viii

Part One: The Career Problem

1. The Career Challenge. 3
2. An Inside Look at the Creative Personality . . . 26

Part Two: Possible Solutions

3. Creative Career Choices. 51
4. Compose Your Own Career 71

Part Three: Making It Happen

5. You Can Get There from Here! 91
6. Have an Adventure 113

Appendix: 215 Jobs for Creative and
        Unconventional People. 139

Notes. 197

For Bill and Lois and Bob

Acknowledgements

~~~~~~

MY FIRST ACKNOWLEDGEMENT GOES TO Professor Jerald Forster of the University of Washington, who suggested during a lecture on career counseling that someone should write a career book for Holland's "Artistic" types. It was one of those times in my life that I remember exactly where I was. When I told him I'd like to write such a book, he nurtured the project as my advisor, doing what he could within academe to further my goal. The original idea was Jerald's, and he continued to contribute ideas until the final draft.

I'd like to extend special thanks to the following people whose work has greatly influenced this book: the editors, illustrators, and designers at Ten Speed Press, whose talents helped me turn my ideas into something you might actually want to read; Richard Bolles for his amazing generosity and the model he provides in his book, *What Color Is Your Parachute?* and in his own life; and John Holland, for an elegant and practical theory that gave me a new vision of the work world and my place in it.

I'd also like to thank my husband, my family and friends, and my colleagues at the University of Pittsburgh Counseling Center for their support. Many creative people, both clients and friends, shared with me their experiences and ideas. Many, many people read my manuscript and offered suggestions that improved it. I have arranged all their contributions in a way that I hope is helpful to you, the reader.

If you have ideas you'd like to contribute, please write to me at the following address:

Carol Eikleberry
P.O. Box 77017
Pittsburgh, PA 15215

Introduction *by Richard Nelson Bolles*

~~~~~~

MANY, MANY BOOKS COME ACROSS my reading table each year, but it has been a long time since one of them impressed me so much as this one has.

Carol has set out to illuminate a very perplexing subject—that of the creative or unconventional impulse in us all. And I found her insights quite dazzling. Chapter Two alone is worth the price of the book.

I have found myself thinking again and again on some of the things she says. She has struck some deep chords with me.

The reason for this lies in the nature of language. Language is a marvelous invention, when you stop to think about it. Take the English language, for example. It uses just twenty-six symbols—which we call the letters of the alphabet—to describe *everything*. Millions and millions of things. All labeled or recalled with the aid of those twenty-six symbols.

A man named John Holland has gone the English language one better. He has invented an alphabet of just six symbols, to describe over 12,000 occupations and their multiple job titles. John's alphabet has become the most popular system for describing occupations existing in the world today. Over 15 million copies of his *Self-Directed Search*, which enshrines that alphabet, have now been purchased and used.

The most significant difference between John's alphabet and the English alphabet, however, has nothing to do with numbers. It is the fact that in the English language the symbols themselves are used without any deep analysis of each symbol. In John's alphabet, the six symbols (R, I, A, S, E, and C) are fraught with meaning and significance, and cry out for analysis. Over the years, that examination has been made, but it is safe to say that the least examined and least understood of John's alphabet—until now—has been the letter *A*—for Artistic.

Since A not only stands for a number of occupations, but also for a gift which potentially lies within us all—the creative impulse—the examination is long overdue.

Here are some of Carol's insights in this book which have particularly impressed me (I state them as I have digested them, rather than in their pristine Carolinian form):

The essence of art or creativity lies in an unusual sensitivity to some aspect of everyday sensory experience, and this sensitivity is something we were born with.

The sensitivity is usually restricted to one area, rather than constituting sensitivity to everything.

The sensitivity may be to pictures, sounds, language, movement, human behavior values (truth, honesty), or whatever. If you are not sure what your sensitivity is, "think about the kinds of ugliness that most distress you."

A person's particular sensitivity brings them both pleasure and pain. "An artistic sensitivity to something combines the potential for a sublime experience with the agony of daily confrontation with the ordinary."

In going about their work, Artistic types prefer to use intuition, which looks for what the senses don't pick up and, most particularly, for the relationships between facts rather than just for the facts themselves.

This tends to lead them to awareness of what is wrong, within their arena of sensitivity. Therefore, creativity begins not with problem-solving, but with "problem-finding"—with the seeing or sensing of a problem. Creative people focus "on what is wrong, what is missing, what needs to be changed to make something better."

An while the emphasis is on problem-finding, as it turns out, "the way a problem is set up often suggests the resolution."

"Very often, the Artistic person is an appreciator rather than a creator...If it is hard to make your living by creating (there were seven times as many artistic types as there were artistic jobs in 1990), it is doubly hard to make your living by appreciating."

This is just a sampler of the wealth of insights to be found in this book.

And what does all this have to do with job-hunting? Well, in a highly competitive job market, often the key to success is first sitting down and thoroughly trying to understand yourself—before you go *out there*. Knowing who you are and what you have to offer is crucial. Carol has made an important contribution indeed to this self-understanding.

—RICHARD BOLLES
August, 1995

PART ONE

The Career Problem

There's no money in poetry,
but then there's no poetry in money, either.

—ROBERT GRAVES

The Career Challenge

WHEN I WAS IN COLLEGE and people talked about "the real world," I thought there was just one real world that was very different from college. Judging from the tone of their voices, I also thought that I probably didn't want to become a part of it. And while I was wrong about the number of real worlds awaiting me, I was right about not wanting to be a part of the first several work worlds I found myself in. The worst was a restaurant in which I worked as a waitress, and even though it was just a temporary job that was helping me meet other goals, I was surprised at how negatively it affected my feelings and self-esteem. My sense of self wasn't as independent of my work environment as I thought it would be.

The college environment had suited me pretty well, and in it I had seen myself as a successful person who was good at her work. I felt like the world was my oyster, and I concluded that because I was a good student, I would be good at most anything. Boy, was I wrong! I was *not* a good waitress—and that was as obvious to me as it was to everybody around me.

Once I knocked a glass of ice water over in a man's lap and stood there dumbfounded while the man's face turned red and my face turned red and the manager and the maitre d' both rushed up from different directions, apologizing profusely. Another time, five people glowered at me and stalked indignantly out of the restaurant because, after waiting for half an hour, I still had not given them their menus. The bartender was always chiding me because instead of paying attention and garnishing the drinks right after he made them, I daydreamed. I was either bored out of my mind or stressed by too many things to do at once. Waitressing was a painful contrast to my performance in college, and I responded by becoming a bit depressed and paralyzed. It took years before I could go into a restaurant without reliving that awful experience.

Now that I better understand myself and the world of work, I can better explain why I was so miserable. I am much more adept working with words than with things, much more accomplished juggling abstract concepts than dishes and glasses, much more interested in talking intimately with people about what troubles them than in taking orders for the number of olives they'd like in their martini.

After waitressing I worked as a receptionist in a doctor's office and found that almost as unpleasant. Then I taught English in college. Teaching English had been my original goal, but it turned out not to be what I thought it would be, so I returned to school to study psychology and creativity and career counseling. Now I'm licensed as a psychologist, and my work counseling people with personal and career concerns fits me very well. But my career is still changing. I'm ready to leave the counseling center where I have worked for the last five years for the scary world of self-employment, and I'm adding a new sideline, writing and giving speeches on my favorite topics in psychology.

Although my career is now going the way I want it to go, my earlier experiences have left me with a profound appreciation for all the different worlds out there and how painful and confusing it can be when the one you work in just doesn't fit. To a large degree, we can choose which kind of work world we want to live in—and it is worth choosing carefully, for our choices affect not only how we spend the best part of our adult lives, but how we feel about ourselves, the kind of people we work with, how much money we make, and how much opportunity we have to make a creative contribution.

This book was written to help people who have the same kinds of problems with their careers that I have had with mine. An idealistic liberal arts major who never wanted to fit into the business world, I disliked most of my jobs and burned out fast. I had a harder time finding work than my friends who went into accounting or engineering or sales, and I also made significantly less money than they did at first. I found it a lot easier to say what I didn't want to do than what I did want to do. But I knew that I wanted to use my brain, to have some autonomy, to make a difference.

I have a special desire to help people who, like me, don't fit easily into conventional doctor or lawyer or banker molds, people who aren't sure exactly what they want to do, and often find that when they begin to describe it in general terms, others are quick to tell them that their ideas are not possible or not practical, people who value personal growth at least as much as money and security and prestige, people who want work that allows them some opportunity for self-expression, and enough freedom and flexibility that they can do things their own way instead of the way it's always been done before.

At this point I know a lot more than I did when I was fresh out of college with my brand-new degree in English, looking for a job. I have learned from my own experience, from the experience of friends, from studying psychology, and from helping clients choose and change careers. I'd like to share with you what I now know, to make your own journey quicker and easier and a little more fun. Think of me as your companion and guide, walking along beside you with a knapsack. In my knapsack I have some useful maps, gifts given to us by brilliant people who have already traveled the territory we are about to enter. We will use our maps with the full appreciation that they are maps and not the territory itself. I will only pull them out when we get to the place where I think they will be most useful. Once they have helped us, we will roll them up and put them back in the knapsack, for, although they are wonderful guides, they were never meant to be taken for reality. No, we must each go into reality on our own feet, noticing some things and not others, responding in our own unique ways. And by the end of the book, we will have reached the end of the territory that I know, and I will say good-bye and you will continue on, on your own.

An Overview

Before we get started, let me pull out the first map. This map was drawn by Lee Roy Beach, a professor and writer and researcher on the subject of decision-making. He calls it *image theory,* and I have used it to organize this book. It's a kind of map of the book you are about to read, an overview that will help you decide where to begin. Because, you know, you might not want to begin at the beginning. You might want to begin with that part of the book that deals with where you are right now.

According to Beach, we tend to make decisions as follows: first, we survey the situation to figure out what's wrong; then, we decide what we are going to do about it; finally, we take action. You go through a similar thinking process when you make a career decision:

- When you choose or change careers, you start by focusing your attention on the relevant parts of the situation, namely, yourself and the world of work. This can be a confusing time if you don't know what parts of yourself and what parts of the work world to focus on. I can help you with that.

- Next, you decide what you are going to do about the situation. What kind of work do you want to do? What are the possibilities? This is both an exciting and a scary time, as you look into lots of possiblities, gather information from people and printed sources, consider pros and cons, perhaps learn of opportunities you never knew existed.

- Finally, having made a choice or choices, you make changes. This is actually the hardest part for most people, because it requires giving up security and taking risks for something that may not work out. It also requires tenacity, and we are not consistent creatures by nature. We often say we are going to do something virtuous, like switch to a new and better occupation—and then don't do it.

As it turns out, Beach's model is both linear and circular, because you don't go through this process just once. The average person changes careers five to seven times; creative and unconventional people will probably change more often than that. So you can expect to circle back through, again and again. You'll figure out what's wrong, make choices or set new goals, and then try to make them happen. And sometimes when you take action, you'll learn something new about yourself or the world of work that causes you to start over.

So, I designed this book in three parts:

- The first section is the "What's going on?" part. Here you will get a bird's eye view of the world of work and learn how people and jobs don't match up. You will also be offered some insights on the creative personality. I hope this section will provide perspective and validation: you may have had trouble with your career, for good reasons that are no fault of your own, but you still have something unique and valuable to offer.

• Part two deals with with career choices. It describes an abundance of work-related possibilities, a variety of possible employers, and many different ways to arrange work in a creative lifestyle. All these options increase your hope for the future and your confidence that you can compose a career that is creative as well as financially realistic.

• Part three focuses on taking action. It suggests practical strategies for turning your dreams into reality and offers a process perspective on developing yourself through creative work. It highlights persistence and courage, which are just as important as talent if you want to apply your creativity to making a living.

Now let's put away Beach's decision-making map and begin our journey...

Personality Types

The world of work is so vast and complicated that it is easy to go into information overload and become overwhelmed when we try to make a career decision. What we need is a new map that will simplify this world enough so that we can begin to understand it. Fortunately, someone has already prepared one. His name is John Holland, and he is a psychologist and researcher who has devoted his lifetime to helping people choose careers. Holland's theory is based on forty years of research with thousands of people in over 400 studies. It is an elegantly simple approach that has been helpful to millions of people all over the world. I believe his map is the best available.

According to Holland's map, there are **six basic personality types** in the world of work, and **six basic work environments.** The idea is to go into a work environment that most closely fits your personality. So before you even start looking for work, you assess your own personality. You can begin right now, by comparing your interests to Holland's six model types.

The following interest test will give you an idea of whether or not you are an Artistic type, according to Holland's framework. You can indicate interest in a occupation even if you don't know much about it and even if you don't have the skills or credentials required. You're not making any commitments now, just noting possibilities. Count the total number of check marks, indicating interest, in each section and compare across the groups. When you are finished, read the descriptions of Holland's six personality types that follow.

Put a check mark by each occupation that interests you:

Artistic

____ Actor

____ Architect

____ Author

____ Dancer

____ Editor

____ Graphic designer

____ Interior designer

____ Photographer

____ Singer

____ Sculptor

____ *Total for Artistic*

Social

____ Clergy member

____ Companion

____ Counselor

____ Nurse

____ Occupational therapist

____ Playground director

____ School principal

____ Social worker

____ Teacher

____ YWCA/YMCA director

____ *Total for Social*

Enterprising

____ Executive

____ Funeral director

____ Lawyer

____ Manager

____ Politician

____ Realtor

____ Retailer

____ Salesperson

____ Stockbroker

____ TV producer

____ *Total for Enterprising*

Realistic

____ Farmer

____ Forester

____ Machinist

____ Mechanic

____ Pilot

____ Plumber

____ Police officer

____ Rancher

____ Repairperson

____ Soldier

____ *Total for Realistic*

Investigative

____ Actuary

____ Computer programmer

____ Dentist

____ Mathematician

____ Optometrist

____ Pharmacist

____ Physician

____ Research scientist

____ Surveyor

____ Veterinarian

____ *Total for Investigative*

Conventional

____ Accountant

____ Banker

____ Cashier

____ Clerk

____ Computer operator

____ Medical record technician

____ Receptionist

____ Secretary

____ Tax preparer

____ Telephone operator

____ *Total for Conventional*

9

The Artistic Type
(a.k.a. Creative and Unconventional)

The Artistic type prefers unstructured work environments in which there is opportunity for self-expression. Artistic people describe themselves as being creative and unconventional and having ability with art, music, drama, or language. (Some very talented Artistic types possess ability in several different areas.) They like to solve problems by creating new products or processes. They are attracted to jobs in the fine arts, such as musician, actor, sculptor, dancer, or writer. However, they are also attracted to applied fields, such as commercial art, interior design, industrial design, journalism, and copywriting. Well-known Artistic types include Pablo Picasso, Laurie Anderson, Frank Lloyd Wright, and Maya Angelou.

There is a great range within the Artistic spectrum, from the person with great talent to those people who appreciate the arts but don't believe they possess any gifts. People with great talents, nascent DaVincis and Mozarts, do not need as much help with their careers as the rest of us. If they are lucky enough to be recognized and nurtured, their path is pretty clear. But if you are not sure what your calling is, or if you have many talents, none of them towering, it's harder to figure out what to do.

The Social Type

The Social type is like the Artistic in that both types are likely to be idealistic and in touch with their feelings. However, the Social type is more likely to prefer working with people. The Social person desires a work environment in which there is opportunity to train, heal, enlighten, or minister to others. They like to solve problems by helping others via feelings or intuition. They describe themselves as being understanding and popular and having ability in teaching and human relations. Social types are attracted to such jobs as teacher, minister, social worker, speech pathologist, nurse, and counselor. Well-known Social types include Mother Teresa, Oprah Winfrey, Barbara Bush, and Mr. Rogers.

The Enterprising Type

The Enterprising type is more like the Social than the Artistic. Like Social types, Enterprising types are sociable and skilled at communication and group leadership. However, their focus is more to influence or persuade than to be helpful. Typically, their goals are to make money or run the organization. They like to solve problems by managing others and taking risks themselves. Enterprising types describe themselves as being dominant and confident and having ability in leadership and sales. They are attracted to jobs such as manager, director, executive, retailer, buyer, promoter, salesperson, and politician. Well-known Enterprising types include Donald Trump, Hillary Clinton, Ted Turner, and Lee Iacocca.

11

The Investigative Type

The Investigative type is like the Artistic in that both types like to work with ideas; both are independent and introspective and like to work alone. However, Investigative people prefer work environments in which there is opportunity to observe and analyze things in order to understand and control them. Investigative types like to solve problems by thinking in an abstract, analytical, task-oriented way. They describe themselves as being scholarly and intellectual and having ability in science and math. They are attracted to jobs such as chemist, biologist, physicist, mathematician, physician, dentist, and college professor. Well-known Investigative types include Albert Einstein, Marie Curie, Linus Pauling, and Nancy Drew.

The Realistic Type

The Realistic type is more like the Investigative than the Artistic. Like the Investigative person, the Realistic type likes to work alone and to work with things; however, they prefer their fields that are more concrete, such as manual work involving tools or machines. Less intellectual than their Investigative counterparts, they like to solve problems by doing something physical with their hands or bodies. Often, Realistic types are rugged, robust people who enjoy the outdoors. They describe themselves as athletic and mechanically inclined. They are attracted to jobs such as farmer, rancher, miner, soldier, plumber, electrician, and pilot. Well-known Realistic types include Martina Navratilova, Amelia Earhart, Mario Andretti and Bob Vila.

The Conventional Type

The Conventional type is, of all the types, the least like the Artistic: Artistic types prefer unstructured work environments in which they can express themselves; Conventional types prefer an orderly work structure to which they can conform. Often Conventional types do the office work necessary to maintain an organization. Someone else initiates the task and they responsibly carry it out, attending to every detail. They like to solve problems by following established procedures, especially procedures for organizing data. They have ability with numbers and clerical tasks. Their career choices include secretary, banker, accountant, cashier, tax expert, office manager, and computer operator. This means that conventional types rarely become well-known, unless through an accident of birth or marriage, as in the case of Queen Elizabeth II or Pat Nixon.

At this point, you might look back to the short interest test you took (on pages 8–9) and see how your answers there compare to the personality types described above.

Vocational psychologist Mark Savickas illustrates how the six types differ from each other by describing how each would approach the problem of a flat tire. Artistic types would express their feelings and then search for novel ways to change the tire. Social types would call up a friend and ask for help. Enterprising types would pay someone else to fix the tire. Investigative types would try to figure out what caused the flat. They might analyze the situation but not necessarily *do* anything about it. Realistic types would get out the appropriate tools and change the tire. Conventional types would pull out the auto club cards they keep up to date and in the glove compartment.

A hexagon best illustrates the relationships of the types to each other. The types closest to each other on the hexagon have the most in common; those across the hexagon from each other are the most dissimilar. Artistic types usually share more interests with Investigative and Social types and have the least in common with Conventional personalities. For example, Artistic and Investigative types share an interest in ideas; Artistic and Social types tend to be in touch with their feelings.

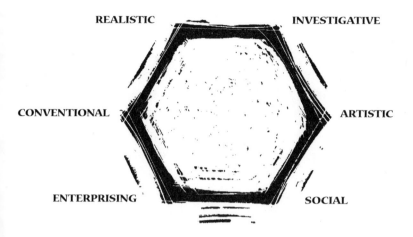

REALISTIC   INVESTIGATIVE

CONVENTIONAL   ARTISTIC

ENTERPRISING   SOCIAL

13

At this point, you're probably saying, "Gee, I see a little of myself in all of these types." And you are right. Few people are truly pure types. Usually people identify two or three of the types as being most like them; sometimes they are more comfortable identifying the one or two types that are the *least* like them. You might ask yourself which two to four of the types you most closely resemble. For the remainder of this book, all you really need to know is which of the other Holland types, in addition to Artistic, best describe your personality. In my case, I know that I'm some combination of Artistic, Investigative, and Social, and that's precise enough for me.

If you would like to take a test so you know for sure which types you most closely resemble, you could call Psychological Assessment Resources at 1-800-331-TEST and ask them to mail you a specimen kit of the Self-Directed Search, written by John Holland. It will cost you about ten dollars, including shipping. The specimen kit includes a test booklet designed to assess your personality according to the theory. After you complete the Self-Directed Search, you will know your three-letter Holland code, composed of the first letter of the three types you most closely resemble. For example, if you resemble Artistic the most, Social the next most, and Enterprising the next most, then your Holland code would be ASE.

Finding a Good Fit

According to Holland's theory, work environments are also Artistic, Investigative, Realistic, Social, Enterprising, or Conventional. An Artistic work environment is one that is dominated by Artistic personalities, meaning that most of the workers in that occupation are Artistic types. Most of the workers in an Investigative jobsite would test out as being Investigative types, and so on

Although there will always be variation in any occupational group, most accountants are Conventional, most sales managers Enterprising, most scientists Investigative, and so on. This is useful information, because one consistent finding in career research is that people like to work with people like themselves, people who share their interests, values, and abilities. As the saying goes, birds of a feather flock together. Many career counselors try to help their clients find flocks of the same feather. After assessing their clients' personality types, they suggest careers dominated by people of like type. Social types are encouraged to consider Social jobs, Artistic types Artistic jobs, and so on. Once you know which two to four types you most closely resemble, you can start looking at the occupations that appeal to people of your type on your own.

In fact, Holland and his associate Gary Gottfredson have given us a detailed map of the work territory: more than 12,000 occupations in the *Dictionary of Occupational Titles* have been analyzed and given a three-letter Holland code. For example, the job of being a reporter is coded ASE, which means it is Artistic first, Social second, and Enterprising third. According to the theory, then, this job would be ideal for those whose Holland code tested out to be ASE. The Career Reference Section in the back of the book includes the Holland codes for most of the careers in the *Dictionary of Occupational Titles* whose first or second letter is *A*. Some of them might seem a little odd or unexpected, but all have components likely to appeal to persons with an artistic or unconventional bent.

Choosing work that fits your personality has a lot to be said for it. For one thing, research shows that if people choose work based on similar interests with coworkers, they are more likely to feel happy and successful at their jobs and less likely to make career changes later in their lives. (The converse is also true: If people choose work in which their

interests are unlike their colleagues, they are more likely to feel dissatisfied and to switch to work more congenial to their personality.)

My own career history illustrates this point. You may remember that
I was miserable as a waitress and only a little less miserable as an office
receptionist. The code for waitress is CES and the code for receptionist
is CSE. I kept the waitressing job for a short time and the receptionist job
a little longer. Then Holland's theory helped me choose my current
work, which provides a good overlap with my Artistic, Investigative, and
Social tendencies. The code for counseling psychologist is SIA; the code
for career counselor is SAE; and the code for writer is AIE. You'll note
that the three-letter match doesn't have to be perfect.

The Mismatch

Finding a career that fits your personality therefore seems both reasonable
and, relatively speaking, easy to achieve. In fact, it would be if there were
enough matching jobs to go around. Unfortunately, the occupational
world is not so ideal. In the United States, at least, the job market is heav-
ily biased toward the left side of Holland's hexagon. There are many more
Realistic and Enterprising jobs than there are Investigative, Artistic, and
Social jobs.

Artistic jobs are especially scarce: Only about 1.5 percent of the U.S. civilian labor force was employed in Artistic occupations in 1990. At the same time, about 9 percent of American men and 13 percent of American women were classified as Artistic. This means that there were about **seven times as many Artistic types as there were Artistic jobs** in 1990. If you've had trouble finding paid creative work, it's no wonder! You were up against a stacked deck.

As you can see, it is harder for an Artistic type than for any of the other personality types to find matching work. Realistic, Conventional, and Enterprising types are lucky, in that they have more jobs to choose from and fewer people to compete with. Investigative and Social types face more competition, but it is nothing like the competition for Artistic jobs.

There is also a gender difference, with more Artistic women than Artistic men. For every three Artistic men, there are more than four Artistic women. Since the percentage of people employed in Artistic occupations is approximately 1.5 percent for both sexes, there are a greater number of Artistic women unable to find a good fit. In fact, women are less likely than men to have a job that fits their personality, regardless of their type. For example, twice as many women are employed in Conventional jobs as aspire to such work.

In African-American, Hispanic, and Native-American groups, Artistic men outnumber Artistic women. About 14 percent of these minority male populations are Artistic, while their female counterparts average between 7 and 10 percent. In the Asian-American population, however, the gender difference is reversed: only 6 percent of Asian men but more than 20 percent of Asian women are Artistic.[1] For all, Artistic job opportunities remain about 1.5 percent.

If these data are discouraging to you, let me offer a word of encouragement. Although the creative role will probably always be a minority function in any culture, the world of work has changed and promises to continue to change in ways that will benefit unconventional people. There are more Artistic work opportunities today than there were twenty-five years ago. Back then, the mismatch was even more extreme, with ten Artistic types for every Artistic job. And the emerging information age promises even greater opportunity for creative people.

Chapter 3 contains more information on the predicted changes in the world of work—changes that promise hope for you. For now, you can comfort yourself with the knowledge that there is an increasing world-wide demand for creative services and products. And the developing job market is open to alternative ways of working, such as job-sharing, temping, and working from home. As the conventional lifetime 9-to-5 job with one employer becomes less the norm, the new work world presents great opportunities to unconventional people who are flexible and independent and eager to learn.

17

Practical Problems

While the future promises hope, some very real and practical problems remain for unconventional people who want to do creative work. These problems, more than any other thing, prompted me to write this book. Career counselors often find that Artistic types are the hardest kind of person to help, because their interests often don't point them toward secure and well-compensated employment. Occupations classified as primarily Artistic generally have had a poor employment outlook and less than average job security.

You probably already know that careers in the fine arts are fiercely competitive and seldom lucrative. A survey of more than 4,000 visual, literary, and performing artists found that, in 1988, most of them earned less than $3,000 from their work. More than 75 percent worked at other jobs to support themselves.[2] However, it's not that grim for everyone—employment prospects for more mainstream Artistic careers are more hopeful.

The following chart provides current information on thirteen Artistic occupations.

OCCUPATION	OUTLOOK	JOB SECURITY	AVERAGE SALARY
Actor/actress	Mixed	Less than average	Variable
Fine artist	Poor	Less than average	Variable
Writer/author	Poor	Less than average	$28,000-$41,000
Art teacher	Mixed	Average	$36,500
Architect	Mixed	Less than average	$39,000-$51,000
Graphic designer	Fair	Less than average	$31,000-$103,000
Musician/singer	Poor	Less than average	Variable
Dancer	Mixed	Less than average	Variable
Interior designer	Good	Less than average	$46,000
Photographer	Mixed	Less than average	$31,500
English teacher	Mixed	More than average	$36,000
Copywriter	Poor	Less than average	$36,000-$72,000
Journalist	Poor	Less than average	$36,000

You will notice that the job outlook for most of these jobs is iffy, and that the salary for some of them is so variable that it is hard to report a meaningful average figure. Salaries for actors are a good example. Off-Broadway stage actors' weekly salaries begin at $340; Broadway actors' weekly salaries begin at $950; television actors earn a weekly rate of $1,685; and Barbra Streisand made $350,000 per week for her work in *All Night Long*.

Variability in other Artistic fields is also extreme. Church musicians make $6,500 to $25,500 a year, but Michael Jackson made $125 million in 1988-1989. Established authors may be paid $5,000 to $15,000 for their novels, but Judith Krantz earned more than $3 million for *Princess Daisy* in reprint fees alone. The average yearly salary for television anchorpersons is $55,000 in smaller cities and $250,000 in larger cities, but Dan Rather earns $2.5 million.[3]

So it goes for Artistic careers. Most of the people employed in creative and unconventional careers earn a decent but moderate salary, while a small number are destitute and an even smaller number become rich and famous. For every Judith Krantz or Barbra Streisand are thousands more aspiring to the top position. Considering the mismatch between the number of Artistic types and the number of Artistic job opportunities, it's no surprise that entry into creative fields is competitive—sometimes keenly competitive.

Emotional Consequences of a Mismatch

It is easy to speculate that the psychological health of creative people would improve if a good job fit were easier to achieve. Although limited data pertain specifically to Artistic types, a good job-personality fit has been found in a number of studies to be positively related to self-esteem, mental health, and life satisfaction. This means that self-esteem, mental health, and life satisfaction are significantly higher for people whose work environment fits their personality type. It has also been found that college students whose major matches their Holland code show better personal adjustment than nonmatching students. While causal links between job fit and mental health are not clear, one study of employees' mental health concluded: "Career and work satisfaction emerged as the strongest contributors to mental health."[4]

One of the best parts of having a job that fits your personality is the opportunity to work with birds of a feather. Just as it is agreeable to be with others who share your outlook on the world, it can feel awful to be an oddball. Media anthropologist Susan Allen says, "The notion that we should be like everyone else, even in this most individualistic of cultures, is immensely strong—and, among the fanatical of any persuasion, it is rigid. Kermit the Frog had it right when he sighed, 'It's not easy being green.'"[5]

It's not easy being an Artistic type employed on the wrong side of Holland's hexagon, either. Occasionally someone who is different is appreciated and valued for his or her uniqueness. Most commonly, though, an Artistic type in a non-Artistic environment feels like the ugly duckling. Others see them not as a swan out of place, but as a bad duck. In the restaurant, my fellow waitresses didn't respect me because my performance was poor, and they couldn't see that I had other strengths. While I found my lack of social status there unpleasant, it was nothing compared to the scapegoating that can happen when people are different. Being considered bad is better than being completely ignored. As African-American writer Ralph Ellison pointed out in *Invisible Man*, the majority culture often denies that the minority individual exists at all. Among all human experiences, the invalidation that comes from not being seen, not being recognized, is among the most painful.

Due to a lack of attractive career options, many creative and unconventional Americans have taken jobs well below their abilities and education. They have been **under**employed. In the last twenty years, competition has been especially fierce for the best-paid jobs, Artistic or otherwise. New jobs just couldn't keep up with the number of job-

seekers. However, underemployment is now decreasing for college grad-
uates: It used to be that one in five college grads was underemployed;
soon it is predicted to be only one in twenty.[6] This is good news for
Artistic types, who tend to be college educated.

Underemployment is often accompanied by poor mental health. One
major study found that underutilization of abilities is positively related to
job dissatisfaction, low self-esteem, and depression.[7] When people had
more education than was required to perform their jobs, they experienced greater boredom, job dissatisfaction, physical complaints, and
depression than people whose education fit their jobs.[8]

Perhaps the best way to sum up is to say that the creative person just
does not fit in in the average work setting. Since psychological adjustment is defined in part as the ability to fit in, it's not too surprising to
learn that Artistic types as a group demonstrate the least confidence
and the greatest psychological distress of all six types. Again and again,
the findings from psychological and vocational studies indicate that
interests in art, music, and literature are associated with more neurotic
problems.

"A healthy, decent man never acts,
paints, writes, or composes."

— THOMAS MANN

Among people with esthetic interests, men are more likely than
women to show signs of emotional distress. Some explanation may be
found in the double standard our society has for artistic pursuit: It's okay
for women but not for men—at least not unless the man happens to be
very successful. A male actor I knew once described with some bitter-
ness how hard it was for him to admit he was an actor, because he experienced instant disrespect for not being a Robert Redford or a Harrison
Ford.

After all this discussion of the emotional consequences of being an
unconventional person in a conventional work world, you might like to
know how well your present job matches your personality. The following questionnaire can help you determine your current fit.

The more items you answered positively ("yes" or "most"), the better fit you already have. The more items you answered negatively, the more you need to consider what you can do to find a better fit. The rest of this book can help you with that task.

Research in social psychology shows that people underestimate the influence of the environment on their behavior, but, as I have indicated, your work environment is likely to be more important than you think and to greatly affect your feelings and self-esteem. If you don't fit in within your current work situation, take heart in knowing that a change in your work environment can make a tremendous difference. The good news is that your workplace is much easier to change than your personality.

Your mental health may be improved just by knowing that there is a theory that explains some of your unpleasant work experiences. Here's what one career workshop participant wrote on an evaluation form after first learning of Holland's theory:

> Oh happiness! I'm greatly relieved to see that an unconventional, independent, creative person with original tendencies fits in some place on the globe. I worried that I didn't like to follow rules and preferred working alone, thought I was doomed to wander the earth unfulfilled and only partially happy.

The theory gave her a new perspective on her career problems and hope for finding a way through them.

Does Your Job Fit Your Personality?

I like my coworkers.	Few	Some	Most	All
People I work with share my values.	Few	Some	Most	All
People I work with respect my skills.	Few	Some	Most	All
My job utilizes my abilities.	Yes	No	Somewhat	
My job utilizes my education.	Yes	No	Somewhat	
My job is related to my interests.	Yes	No	Somewhat	
At work I work on problems I think are important.	Yes	No	Somewhat	
I am proud of the role I play at work.	Yes	No	Somewhat	
I am able to express myself at work.	Yes	No	Somewhat	
At work I am rewarded for being who I am, financially and/or through personal appreciation.	Yes	No	Somewhat	

*"An artist is not a special kind of person.
Every person is a special kind of artist."*

—Meister Eckhart

~~~~~~~~~~~~~~~~

*"A work of art is a corner of creation seen
through a temperament."*

—Emile Zola

An Inside Look at the Creative Personality

IN THE LAST CHAPTER WE LEARNED that creative people don't fit in within the average work environment. In this chapter we will look more closely at the ways creative people don't fit, and I will try to help you see your own unique spin on being different. The better you understand your creative gifts, the better you will be able to attain an unconventional niche for yourself. There is a paradox here, in that the traits that make you different are generally the same traits that make you best fitted for a specific creative job. You **can** fit in if you find the right environment

There is always the temptation to deny or hide our differences, or to spend years trying to change parts of ourselves that we later conclude aren't changeable. I still sometimes resist saying what's on my mind, because I don't like being the one with the strange new ideas that make other people feel uncomfortable. When it comes to your career, though, I believe that the best approach is to understand and accept your differences, and then look for environments in which being the unique person you are is a terrific advantage.

Our next map is one that I have drawn myself with the help of psychologists such as Donald MacKinnon and Mihaly Csikszentmihalyi, experts on creativity. You may not appreciate what a daunting task it is to draw a map of personality. Personality is changing, fluid, ephemeral, inherently contradictory and abstract.

Holland's theory suggests that certain personality characteristics are more likely in some of the types than others. The adjectives listed below are believed to be the best descriptors of each type. Check those adjectives that you think best describe your personality, and then compare across groups once again to see which of the types you most closely resemble—and which you least resemble.

Realistic:

____ asocial

____ conforming

____ frank

____ genuine

____ hard-headed

____ inflexible

____ materialistic

____ natural

____ normal

____ persistent

____ practical

____ self-effacing

____ thrifty

____ uninsightful

____ uninvolved

____ *Total Realistic traits*

Artistic:

____ complicated

____ disorderly

____ emotional

____ expressive

____ idealistic

____ imaginative

____ impractical

____ impulsive

____ independent

____ introspective

____ intuitive

____ nonconforming

____ open

____ original

____ sensitive

____ *Total Artistic traits*

Enterprising:

____ acquisitive

____ adventurous

____ agreeable

____ ambitious

____ domineering

____ energetic

____ exhibitionistic

____ excitement-seeking

____ extroverted

____ flirtatious

____ optimistic

____ self-confident

____ sociable

____ talkative

____ *Total Enterprising traits*

Investigative:

____ analytical

____ cautious

____ critical

____ complex

____ curious

____ independent

____ introspective

____ intellectual

____ pessimistic

____ precise

____ rational

____ reserved

____ retiring

____ unassuming

____ unpopular

____ *Total Investigative traits*

Social:

_____ ascendant

_____ cooperative

_____ friendly

_____ generous

_____ helpful

_____ idealistic

_____ empathic

_____ kind

_____ patient

_____ persuasive

_____ responsible

_____ sociable

_____ *Total Social traits*

Conventional:

_____ careful

_____ conforming

_____ conscientious

_____ defensive

_____ efficient

_____ inflexible

_____ inhibited

_____ methodical

_____ obedient

_____ orderly

_____ persistent

_____ practical

_____ prudish

_____ thrifty

_____ unimaginative

_____ *Total Conventional traits*

27

The adjectives you checked will probably fall into many of the six categories, rather than just one. This is to be expected, because each type is a theoretical ideal that describes no real individual perfectly. In addition, even if you are creative in many ways, you will find that some of the adjectives don't seem to apply to you. Among people that I think are highly creative, I've met some who tell me their creativity is the only thing they feel confident about and others who say they don't even think they are creative. If you feel doubtful about your creativity, try to be open to the possibility of discovering previously unrecognized gifts.

Come with me now as we explore the psyche of the creative person. In personality, psychic phenomena are a complicated holistic jumble, but I will present them in a simple linear sequence for the sake of clarity. We will proceed from the perceptions of the creative person to their thoughts and feelings and finally to their behavior.

Esthetic Sensitivity

Artistically creative people are unusually sensitive to some aspect of their everyday sensory experience. Musicians hear more: their ears detect more subtle distinctions, picking up timbre, overtones, harmonies, and counterpoint where less sensitive listeners may only hear a sound or a single melody. Dancers respond to movement and kinesthetics. Writers are attuned to language. Dramatists have a sensitivity to human behavior.[9]

Such sensitivity begins as an innate talent or gift. This sensitivity may be trained and developed, but the potential must be present at birth. A person who lacks tonal memory won't become a musician. A person who has no eye for balance and proportion can't produce art. And a person who wants to write creatively needs more than a creative writing class, although the teacher will have a place to begin if the student is sensitive to language.

28

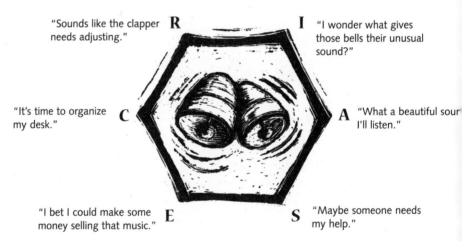

"Sounds like the clapper needs adjusting." **R**

I "I wonder what gives those bells their unusual sound?"

"It's time to organize my desk." **C**

A "What a beautiful sound, I'll listen."

"I bet I could make some money selling that music." **E**

S "Maybe someone needs my help."

Whatever their innate sensitivities may be, artistically creative people are open to perceptual experience. Perceptual means both receiving sensory information, usually from the eyes or the ears, and then organizing that information in the mind. The act of reading this book is a perceptual experience—your eyes pick up little black shapes on a white page, but your mind recognizes the form of letters and words. The diagram illustrates the way the six personality types might respond to the perceptual experience of hearing bells ringing.

Whereas other types respond to the bell ringing by assuming a meaning for the sound, those with artistic sensitivity respond to the sound of the bell itself.[10] In the following passage, artist Georgia O'Keeffe describes her sensitivity and receptivity to the sight of a flower:

> A flower is relatively small. Everyone has many associations with a flower—the idea of flowers. You put out your hand to touch the flower—lean forward to smell it—maybe touch it with your lips almost without thinking—or give it to someone to please them. Still—in a way—nobody sees a flower—really—it is so small—we haven't time—and to see takes time like to have a friend takes time. If I could paint the flower exactly as I see it no one would see what I see because I would paint it small like the flower is small.
>
> So I said to myself—I'll paint what I see—what the flower is to me but I'll paint it big and they will be surprised into taking time to look at it.[11]

29

Like O'Keeffe, most artists value the perceptual experience of sight and communicate their unique vision through their work. It appears to the viewer that the artist has seen something the audience didn't see, or has seen it in a different way. Those members of the audience who are visually sensitive are given pleasure by the work, because viewing it creates a new perceptual experience for them.

> *"It is the function of art to renew our perception.*
> *What we are familiar with we cease to see. The writer*
> *shakes up the familiar scene, and as if by magic,*
> *we see new meaning in it."*
>
> —ANAÏS NIN

Artistic types value esthetics. (In fact, "to perceive" is the root of the word *esthetic*.) They are likely to give appreciating beauty the same degree of value that an Enterprising type would give to making a profit or a Conventional type would give to keeping the record straight. Whereas the types on the left side of the hexagon would be more likely to value their objets d'art for the status of ownership, Artistic types would be more likely to value it for its intrinsic beauty. Or they might appreciate something beautiful without wanting to own it at all.

Sensitivity to beauty may paradoxically bring pain as well as pleasure. A calligrapher friend of mine once told me that the ugly and ordinary lettering of storefront signs in her neighborhood pained her. Similarly, after refining my appreciation of literature in college, I suffered both as an English teacher and as a psychology student when I was required to read poorly written prose. It is like the wine connoisseur who is confronted with a glass of fermented grape juice.

So it is with any talent or sensitivity possessed to an extreme degree. On the one hand it is wonderful to be able to see and appreciate beauty around you that others may not see at all. On the other hand, this keen sensitivity combines the potential for a sublime experience with the agony of daily confrontation with the ordinary.

I believe that any individual person will be quite sensitive to some perceptual experiences but not to others. Sensitivity varies both within and across individuals. For example, I am more visually sensitive than my husband, and I enjoy watching movies more than he does; he is more sensitive to taste than I am, and he experiences a cup of coffee and a cinnamon roll with a pleasure I envy. For help in recognizing your unique sensitivities, you might look over the following list that was compiled at Richard Bolles's 1994 life/work planning workshop. These are the things the participants came up with when asked what they notice:

What Are You Sensitive to That You Don't Think Everybody Is?

THESE THINGS THAT THEIR EYES PICK UP:

Outer Sight:

Nature:

• The quality of light

• Colors

• Sunset

• Sunrise

• Stars

• A rose opening, flowers

• Pets

Sacred Places and Buildings

Products:

• Artistic objects and antiques

• A photograph developing

Inner Sight:

Nature:

• Visual harmony

• The auras of trees and plants

People:

• Our loved ones, in their element

• Children playing

• Emotions playing on people's faces

• Dancers

• Hand motion

• Beautiful athletes in motion

• Injury

• Flow of energy between people

• Drifting vs. purposeful action

• Sensitivity of other people

• Auras

• Inner voices

• Things about to be broken

• Dangerous people

• Frightening creatures

31

THESE THINGS THAT THEIR EARS PICK UP:

Nature:

• The ocean hitting the shoreline

• Waterfalls

• Birdsongs

• Crickets

• Frogs

• Campfires

• Cats purring

Silence

Songs, music:

• Muzak

People:

• The voices and laughter of loved ones

• Stories

• Blessings

• Words of love and appreciation

THESE THINGS THAT THEIR NOSES PICK UP:

Places:
- A library
- Parents' home

Products:
- Wood shavings
- Leather
- Pipe tobacco
- New car smell

Outdoors:
- Fresh air
- Pine trees
- Fresh cut grass
- Plowed field
- Herbs
- Rain
- Foods

THESE THINGS THAT THEIR MOUTHS PICK UP:

Favorite Foods:
- Berries, berry pie
- Homemade bread
- Homegrown tomatoes
- Chocolate
- Fresh corn
- Japanese rice crackers
- Fresh roasted peanuts

People:
- The kiss of one's beloved

THESE THINGS THAT THEIR HANDS OR BODIES PICK UP:

People:
- Babies
- Quality handshake
- Skin
- Hugs as "harbor"
- The body of the opposite sex

Nature:
- The feel of the wind
- Soil

- The bark of a tree
- Bitter cold or extreme heat
- Petting animals

Products:
- A smooth rock
- Fabrics
- Pages of a book
- Sculpture
- Hand-crafted materials

THESE THINGS THAT THEIR RIGHT BRAIN PICKS UP HOLISTICALLY:

How Space Is Used

Rhythm of the Universe:

- Paradox
- Trends
- Connections
- Possibilities in unrelated things
- Disharmony

33

Recollection in Great Detail of Anything

Let me illustrate how your unique sensitivity could relate to your career. One of my clients was exquisitely sensitive to color, and she used this talent on the job. She was a costume designer who could make 100 costumes come out the identical shade of blue, because she knew by gazing into dye lots exactly how many drops of dye were needed to make a match. And when the art director came to her and said that he wanted a costume "the color of the earth, rich and warm and fecund," she was able to go from his words to a color that sent him into rapture.

In recognizing my creativity, it has helped me to focus on those areas where I am most sensitive. For example, I am sensitive to words and to individual differences, and I am much better at coming up with words for a speech than I am at coming up with ways to distract a fussy baby, and much better at recognizing psychological differences between people than at recognizing pitches in music.

Think about your own areas of sensitivity, and how they differ from other people you know. What kinds of sensory or perceptual experience give you the greatest pleasure? If you are not sure, think about the kinds of ugliness that most distress you. Keep your answers in mind as you read the next section on creativity. You may find that you are most creative in that area or combination of areas where you are most sensitive, whether it is with pictures, sounds, language, movement, human behavior, or whatever.

Creative Thinking Is Intuitive and Divergent

In recent years, researchers of creativity have given as much attention to problems as to solutions. Problem-finding is now thought to be at least as important to creativity as problem-solving. "The creative process," wrote psychologist Donald MacKinnon, "starts always with the seeing or sensing of a problem. The roots of creativeness lie in one's becoming aware that something is wrong, or lacking, or mysterious. One of the salient traits of a truly creative person is that he sees problems where others don't..."[12]

"There is something mechanical, as it were,
in the art of finding solutions. The truly original
mind is that which finds problems."

—PAUL SOURIAU

Problem-finding means that you approach your area of sensitivity in an open, playful way, without preconceived ideas or stereotyped problems already in mind. Not fully conscious of a goal, you explore, experiment, and discover as new problems emerge or reveal themselves. The process of finding new problems is a kind of curiosity-driven learning in which problems lead gradually to solutions, since the way a problem is set up often suggests the resolution.

Intuition is involved with both discovering and solving problems. Intuition is an unconscious perceptual process that picks up on potential problems and possible solutions. The mysterious process of intuition is thought to be a creative way of perceiving, wherein you unconsciously search beyond the reality presented to your senses for deeper, more meaningful possibilities. It's a way of discerning what the senses don't pick up.

According to the psychologist Carl Jung, sensation is a perceptive process that focuses on actuality—the facts—whereas intuition is a process that focuses on possibility—the relationships between the facts. It's the difference between what is and what could be, between reality as it is commonly accepted, and the discovery of previously unexplored potentialities.

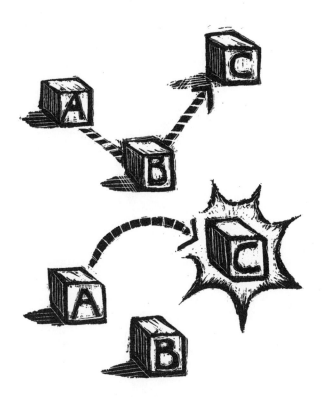

Sensory thinking is usually linear: A leads to B leads to C. Intuitive thinking, on the other hand, is more likely to occur in leaps, leaving you as an intuitive thinker unsure of how you reached your conclusion: A leads to C, and you are not aware of bypassing B. Often this is experienced as the excitement of a creative insight—the "eureka!" experience.

Think, for example, of Archimedes, who had been struggling for a way to measure volume. It is unlikely that when he sat down in the bathtub he thought, "My body in the tub is like any body in water; the rise of the water is a way of measuring the volume taken up by any object; I have found a way to measure volume." It is more likely that his "eureka!" preceded his step-by-step analysis.

We all use both sensation and intuition as ways of picking up information from the world around us. However, each of us tends to prefer one mode over the other, to achieve greater strength in the preferred mode, and to engage in it more often. While there are exceptions, Artistic types show a strong preference for intuition. Opposite them on the hexagon, Conventional types show a strong preference for sensation.

Creative and unconventional people often see problems and come up with solutions that others don't. Their intuitions may seem flaky or off-the-wall to the more forthright and practical sensing person. Some strongly intuitive creative people may occasionally feel misunderstood and unfairly judged as lacking in intellectual ability by their more linear and left-brained colleagues.

36

Once creative thinkers have found a problem, they solve it by generating lots of ideas. They use **divergent thinking.** (IQ tests measure *convergent* thinking: the ability to pick a single right answer to a given problem.) Divergent thinking, like intuition, is considered an important aspect of creativity. (Creativity researchers call it fluency. The Johnson O'Connor Research Foundation, an organization that tests human aptitudes, calls it ideaphoria.) It is the ability to come up with many possible solutions to a problem for which there is no single right answer.

An example of a question on a divergent thinking test might be something like: "What would happen if all the water in the world were suddenly to freeze?" or "How many different ways can you use a brick?" Divergent thinkers would be able to come up with many more answers to these kinds of questions than convergent thinkers.

A visual example of a question from a divergent thinking test is shown on page 36. If you were taking the test you would be asked to include the given line in your own drawing of something that no one else would think of and to "keep adding new ideas to your first idea" until you had developed a picture that told an interesting story.

Divergent ideas may be plentiful but not particularly appropriate. For example, one of my creative friends had countless ideas for my career that I found unappealing, such as caring for orangutans in New Guinea, mass-marketing trout from my remote mountain cabin, and interviewing customers on video to help them create their own video diaries. Divergent thinkers may look a little crazy and farfetched to their friends whose thinking is more convergent, because it is likely that many of their ideas won't work. But this is all part of the creative process. After all, at one time it was absurd to think the world might be round. We tend to forget that the few ideas that are socially valued evolved out of a process in which many less appropriate ideas were abandoned.

"Civilization is a slow process of adopting
the ideas of minorities."

—HERBERT PROCHNOW

The divergent thinker's ability to come up with a great many ideas increases the likelihood that at least some of the ideas will be appropriate. In the arts, creators are often advised to "kill their darlings"—to cut out parts that do not fit into the whole, even though they may be very attached to them. Obviously, you need plenty of ideas so you can cut freely and still have something left. And you still need the help of convergent thinking. Divergent thinking will ensure many possibilities; convergent thinking will help you choose the one best solution to the problem.

Compared to the more simple, concrete, and literal thinking of the types on the left side of Holland's hexagon, the thinking of the Artistic type tends to be complex, abstract, and symbolic. Once they have perceived something in their open and sensitive way, they give new form and meaning to their experience, creating new images and symbols that bring

37

their ideas together in a meaningful and pleasing whole. These original creations clearly belong to their genre and yet seem refreshingly new. Jim Henson's Muppets and Maya Lin's Vietnam War Memorial are two good examples of this.

Although I sound very appreciative of divergent thinking, you should know that I yelped when my editor bombarded me with lots of ideas for changing this manuscript. When I expressed my dismay over new ideas not in line with my vision, she said, "My mind tends to leap ahead of the immediate problem, create more problems, and come up with possibilities no one needs or wants. Fortunately an occasional good one creeps in there, too." In fact, she had many ideas that made this a more readable book—and in my opinion she made a good career choice when she became an editor. Chapter 3 discusses editing and many other occupations that require creative thinking.

Emotions Are Expressed, Often Indirectly

Artistic types describe themselves as emotional and expressive, which fits the stereotype of the moody and temperamental artist. While some of their emotion is positive, such as the romantic love celebrated in popular music, much of it is not. In fact, negative emotionality is related to creativity. You may be surprised, because creativity is so often confused with social desirability. After reading many psychological studies of creative people, however, I am struck by how often they are described as possessing traits that are considered socially *un*desirable.

What traits have been used to describe creative and artistic people in psychological studies? Hostile, aggressive, dominant, and self-centered. Histrionic, rebellious, effeminate, and immature. Anxious and insecure; impulsive and emotionally unstable. Undependable, irresponsible, unsympathetic, inconsiderate, and certainly not agreeable. (If you feel offended, you may note that these adjectives reflect the biases of the researchers and a certain amount of immaturity in the subjects. For a look at more mature creativity, see the last chapter in this book.)

The intuitive preference for what could be, rather than what is, helps to produce some of these negative feelings. Creative people often focus on what is wrong, what is missing, what needs to be changed to make something better. In fact, many creative people look like chronic malcontents to outsiders, because they are always searching for what can be improved. On the Strong Interest Inventory, a test commonly used to help students choose careers, the Artistic type checks "dislike" in answer to the test questions more frequently than any other type!

The writer Barker Gray described his dissatisfaction with the status quo as being like irritation at a bell that is off pitch: the truth that others presented to him didn't "sound" true to him, and he would feel driven to discover the truth for himself, but then feel dissatisfied again when his new idea improved part of the sound but left the rest still wrong. He assumed the solution *must* be a new synthesis. For him, the quest for truth involved sensitivity to a conflict between conventional explanations and his own beliefs, and his task as a creator was to internalize and reconcile that conflict.

39

"Of our conflicts with others we make rhetoric; of our conflicts with ourselves we make poetry."

—WILLIAM BUTLER YEATS

Conflict is a word often encountered in psychological explanations of creativity. The very richness and complexity associated with conflict yields a more creative product. The sensitive Artistic person perceives a complex world in which certain elements are wrong or don't fit—and then experiences internal conflict as part of the creative process of reorganizing them. The conflict comes in part because they do not rest content with old forms. Such internal conflict may help produce the emotional state that others perceive as moodiness and histrionics.

"Every act of creation is first of all an act of destruction."

—PABLO PICASSO

"Medicine, to produce health, has to examine disease; and music, to create harmony, must investigate discord."

—PLUTARCH

Writer Jacob Brownowski theorizes that people like Einstein upset the more conventional thinkers because the Einsteins of the world often espouse unusual ideas that are unrelated to their scientific contributions. In the following passage, he imagines how Einstein might respond when asked why he can't just stick to relativity and stay out of politics:

> To that, of course, people like Einstein have always had to reply, 'If I were not a very awkward character, I would not have thought of relativity in the first place.' You do not invent a new world system by being satisfied with what other people have told you about how the world works. And that dissatisfaction goes through and through, and it makes a complete personality.[13]

Critical, challenging, independent—these are characteristics of many creative people. If you are an agent of change, if you question and challenge the status quo, you are likely to be seen as a troublemaker and to make others feel uncomfortable. While it is certainly the case that many creative and unconventional people present their sweet, gentle, agreeable aspects to the world and control or hide their destructive impulses, it is important to realize that creativity has its negative consequences.

Surely other people are also dissatisfied and emotional. They are human beings living in the same imperfect world. But conventional people more frequently suppress or repress the feelings that artistic people express. A psychological understanding of how you deal with anxiety may be helpful here. While being closed and seeing the world in simple and concrete terms may better enable you to manage your anxiety, admitting to yourself a more complex world view may lead to greater anxiety—as well as greater creativity. Many psychological studies have found that creative people are both more anxious and less repressed than "normals." They don't deny that things trouble them.

While creative people often behave in an impulsive and dramatic fashion, they may have difficulty communicating their feelings directly. I remember watching one of my artistic roommates create a work of art for a boyfriend with whom she had fought. Rather than going to him and saying, "I love you and I am sad that I hurt you," she painted him a lovely picture that expressed those feelings. This is what Freud meant when he described the various art forms as sublimation, one of the most mature of the psychological strategies for dealing with anxiety. Sublimation may be understood as an unconscious way of expressing emotion through the distance of art.

Communicating feelings indirectly is part of a tendency to relate to people at arm's length. Creative artists often prefer indirect interpersonal relationships, but that does not mean that these relationships are unimportant to them. The acknowledgement of others may be very important, even catalytic. Super and Crites, vocational researchers, have written: "For the person who wants to remain emotionally uninvolved with people, yet needs their applause, aesthetic activities appear to offer an opportunity to carry on interpersonal relations at a distance while gaining the recognition of others."[14]

David Copperfield, the magician, described it this way in an interview with the *Seattle Times*: "I started doing magic at ten and I had a lot of early success and approval. Magic became something I could do on stage and get paid for. I admired songwriters who could take elements of their lives and express themselves on stage. I try to do the same thing with magic. It's a way to communicate and to express myself." Behind all art seems to lie that basic urge: to communicate not just ideas but the feelings that accompany them, and to do it in a way that will capture the attention and imagination of an audience.

To recognize your own unique spin on creativity, think about how you express yourself. Through which expressive forms are your feelings the most accessible to others? It may be obvious, as it is with mimes like Marcel Marceau, whose work is infused with emotion. But in some creative fields feeling is expressed in less obvious ways. Industrial designers, for example, design cars that are technically functional but that also express such feelings as security or excitement.

Independent and Non-Conforming Behavior

It seems to be a part of human nature that we all want to fit in and stand out at the same time. In creative people, however, the latter urge is much stronger. Creative people assert their individuality. They resist stereotyping. Any theory that categorizes people, including Holland's construct, can be a turn-off. Artistic types don't want so much to be like other Artistic types as they want to be unlike all types.

"Individuality of expression is the beginning and end of all art."

—JOHANN WOLFGANG VON GOETHE

"Art is the most intense mode of individualism that the world has known."

—OSCAR WILDE

Artistic types describe themselves as independent. Their self-sufficient behavior reflects this independence of judgment. One researcher concluded, "A protest against a great deal of parental concern, the desire to be free and untrammeled, to resist superimposed structure and standards, to be nonconformist…can be inferred from high artistic interes…"[15] Not surprisingly, of the six Holland types, the Artistic type is the least influenced by social factors such as what their family, friends, and teachers think. Their career choices are more influenced by what *they* like and are drawn to, often causing family concern that they don't know what they are doing or what is best for them.

Although some creative and unconventional people are so non-conforming that they avoid school completely, many Artistic types are well educated. This is a group that aspires to and achieves a high level of academic status: Master's degrees and doctorates are not uncommon. In fact, it has been found that a person's interest in esthetics increases the longer they engage in formal education. Ideally, a formal, liberal education trains you to think for yourself, freeing you from convention so that you may choose your own path.

In general, creative and unconventional people avoid business and practical courses of study, seeking out the theoretical and abstract. Artistic types major in the fine arts, liberal arts, or humanities. Investigative types, on the other hand, are likely to major in science or engineering; Realistic types, in agriculture (or they may get vocational training or join the military). Social types are likely to end up in colleges of education or social work; Enterprising and Conventional types, in business.

"Divergers are less interested in success, more interested in self-expression. They chose unusual occupations, such as inventor or entertainer, rather than the more conventional doctor or lawyer."

—Leona Tyler

So while the other Holland types pursue degrees that translate readily into actual jobs, creative and unconventional people are likely to take courses that do *not* lead directly to employment, and they may spend extracurricular time in such activities as dance, debate, comedy, photography, or school publications. This academic path is likely to be seen by others as idealistic and impractical. After all, what does one do with a degree in women's studies or oriental philosophy?

43

A high Artistic score on a vocational interest test may be said to reflect an appreciation for the finer things in life. Although the stereotype of the artist is of the creator, very often the Artistic person is an appreciator rather than a creator. In this sense, too, your educational endeavors may be seen as impractical. If it is hard to make your living by creating, it is doubly hard to make your living by appreciating. As I know from personal experience, you can spend many years and thousands of tuition dollars learning to appreciate the great achievements of Western civilization—only to find yourself washing dishes or waiting tables!

Creative people tend to be independent in their relation to authority figures. **They want to do their own thing their own way.** The first time I led a career group for creative and unconventional people, I was struck with the number of group members who described conflict with their bosses as part of their work woes. If you are unconventional, the worst kind of boss is the kind who breathes down your neck and actively supervises your work. Creative people are happier at work, and probably perform better, if they are given their freedom. They value autonomy.

Seen from this perspective, it makes sense that Artistic types would avoid Conventional work, which is in part defined as adhering to a given structure, maintaining the established order, or following explicit directions to accomplish an explicit task. For tasks such as filing, typing, and accounting, which are Conventional in nature, it makes great sense that the worker does the work the way it has always been done. If you are Artistic, though, these kinds of clerical and business duties feel like death to the soul. Not only have you lost your freedom in the 9-to-5 grind, but you have lost all personal freedom in doing the work itself.

A sensitive, intuitive, expressive nature is no advantage when the task is to handle everyday maintenance chores by established rules. In fact, you may find that you are less efficient and more tired by the work than other people would be. Because so many of the jobs that are available are conventional jobs, you may get down on yourself and think, "I just don't like to work." You may not realize that it's just that particular kind of work that's so distasteful to you, not *all* work.

Perhaps the most general descriptive statement about Artistic people is that they prefer unstructured work environments with opportunities for self-expression, as a way to connect emotionally with others, to achieve recognition, and to find personal meaning in a symbolic way. The fine arts provide the purest opportunity for such personal growth.

Consider the following quote from *The Creative Vision*, a study of young art students at the Chicago Art Institute:

> The four major reasons the artists gave for painting or sculpting—discovery in general, self-knowledge, understanding other people, and the quest for reality—are, of course, closely interrelated. Taken together, they seem to point to a deep existential commitment to coming to terms with life. If we are to trust the self-report of artists, this, and not the usual external rewards of a profession, is what motivates them to devote their lives to their vocation.[16]

The usual external rewards of a profession—money, status, and power, for example—motivate the Enterprising, Conventional, and Realistic types more than they do the Artistic type. Of course Artistic people would like to make lots of money and indulge in some luxuries and be treated with deference and respect, but their strongest ambitions are more subtle. It is the opportunity to do the work itself that motivates, given the by-products of self-discovery and personal understanding.

"I don't like work—no man does—but I like what is in work
—the chance to find yourself. Your own reality—
for yourself—not for others—what no other man can ever know."

—JOSEPH CONRAD

45

John Steinbeck referred to this kind of personal motivation for writing when he said, "I can say now that one of the big reasons was this: I instinctively recognized an opportunity to transcend some of my personal failings—things about myself I didn't particularly like and wanted to change but didn't know how." Steven Soderbergh's account of his script for his movie *sex, lies, and videotape* illustrates a similar desire for self-discovery and personal understanding. In an interview with the *Seattle Times*, he said the script was written following his breakup "with someone I behaved really poorly to, someone I was very close to. I was obsessed with how and why that happened, and how I could keep it from happening again."

"A genius is a person who, seeing farther and probing deeper
than other people, has a different set of ethical valuations from theirs,
and has energy enough to give effect to this extra vision and
its valuations in whatever manner best suits
his or her specific talents."

—GEORGE BERNARD SHAW

We have come to the end of our tour of the creative personality, and can now roll up our map having gained a better understanding of what's going on inside you. This map is less action-oriented than the others. You might ask someone who doesn't understand you to read this chapter, and maybe they'll become more tolerant once they realize that it's legitimate for you to be different from them. You may find it easier to explain why you are not happy with the job you now have and to articulate what would make you happier.

I invite you to look at yourself gently and uncritically, searching for connections between your perceptions and thoughts and feelings and actions. The more aware of and the better friends you are with all the different parts of yourself, the better able you will be to integrate them into a unified whole. As a whole person you can act in your own best interest, making choices and engaging in creative work, which is the focus of the next two parts of the book.

VISIONS
DREAMS
SUBLIMATION
THE HORIZON OF UNLIMITED POSSIBILITIES
HILLS OF COMPLEXITY
FOREST OF INTERNAL CONFLICT
The CAVES of MALCONTENT
INTUITION
UNKNOWN OPTIONS
ROAD OF NON-CONFORMITY
PROBLEM-FINDING
PERCEPTUAL EXPERIENCES
ESTHETIC SENSITIVITY
DIVERGENT THINKING

PART TWO

Possible Solutions

"In choosing an occupation one is, in effect, choosing a means of implementing a self-concept."

—DONALD SUPER

Creative Career Choices

HAVING LEARNED ABOUT WHAT'S GOING ON outside in the world of work and inside in your creative self, it's time to ask: If you already have a clear idea of what you want to do, you can skip this chapter. But even if you are already pretty well matched with your current job or course of study, you might like to try on some new ideas or dream a little about different kinds of work.

If you need to decide on a career for the first time or the umpteenth time, let me offer a little guidance. Making choices isn't easy to do. In fact, it feels risky and scary to many people, and in their haste to get it done and behind them, they shortchange the process. They don't consider enough options and then they don't get enough information on the options they are considering, and their choices turn out badly. I will help you now to consider a lot of options, and later you can get more information on the options that are the most attractive to you. Then you can trust your intuition to help you make a good career choice.

Your Skills

Assuming you already know that you have artistic interests and a creative personality, the most important self-knowledge you need to acquire now is knowledge *about* your skills. As we saw in the first part of the book, esthetic interests alone don't necessarily lead to employment. When I help clients choose a career, I usually spend as much time on their skills as I do on their vocational interests. **Interests and skills together point to an occupation**. More than any other factor, your skills help you translate who you are into a job.

Skills are what you *do*, expressed as verbs (like playing, speaking, writing, helping, directing, and so on). They are what you do on the job, and they can be used in any number of different jobs. Your most important skills are talents or aptitudes that you have developed through use. It feels good to use these skills; it may even feel bad *not* to use them. Knowing and using your skills lies at the heart of career development, as the following story illustrates.

One time a fifty-year-old woman who was not happy with her job came to see me for career counseling. I asked her how she saw the problem. The problem, she said, was that she was too young to retire. She was tired of working and ready to retire, but she couldn't afford to. Since she had to work, she wanted whatever she did to be as stress-free as possible. For her this meant no after-hours work. She wanted to leave the job behind at the end of an eight-hour work day to make maximum time for herself.

I asked her to do a skills analysis and recommended the exercise in *What Color Is Your Parachute?* She did the analysis exercise at home, and when she returned to see me for her next appointment, she was a different person. Now that she was more aware of her skills, she saw the problem differently. She said the problem was that her present job as a computer programmer processing office data didn't require her *preferred skills.* Through the skills analysis, she had learned her strength lay in synthesizing visual information. She had even targeted a new career that would allow her to use these skills: programming interactive multimedia computer games. Now that she had identified her true calling, she was excited. It was all right with her if she worked fourteen-hour days, because the work wouldn't feel stressful.

Her story is not unusual. When you do work that fits your skills, you feel less stress. Your dependable strengths, as Bernard Haldane calls them, come naturally to you. These skills seem easy to use, because you don't have to force yourself, or exert great amounts of discipline or willpower. When you work with your natural strengths, you usually enjoy the process and feel you're doing it well. It's like flying with the wind, instead of against it.

Besides helping you identify less-stressful ways to make a living, there are other advantages to knowing your skills. One of them is that focusing on your skills enhances self-esteem. Whether you call them skills, motivated abilities, dependable strengths, talents, or gifts, they are positive things about you. When you use them, you feel good about yourself. When you see that they are part of who you are and that you have used them since your childhood, your confidence grows. You'll develop inner security about your ability to support yourself and to make a meaningful contribution through your skills.

53

When you are aware of your skills, you can be more articulate during your job-hunt. Skills are what employers want to know about. Skills are what you put on your resume and what you talk about in a job interview. When the interviewer says, "Tell me about yourself," you talk about your skills. You say, "I *can* because I *have*. I can do this job because I have done work like this in the past, using skills X, Y, and Z." And then you support your statements with concrete, relevant, detailed stories of accomplishments from your past.

How can you acquire this kind of self-knowledge that gives you direction, decreases your stress, improves your self-esteem, and helps you sell yourself to employers? There are several ways, and I recommend them all.

The best option is to do the skills analysis in *What Color Is Your Parachute?*[17] (also sold separately in a smaller, less expensive booklet called *How to Create a Picture of Your Ideal Job or Next Career*[18]). *The Truth about You*[19] is a useful companion guide. In addition to helping you recognize your favorite skills, *The Truth about You* can help you discover the kinds of problems and rewards that really motivate you. If you are lost and unsure what to do with your life, I can't think of a better way to begin finding a focus than with these two resources.

Both the skills analysis in *Parachute* or *How to Create a Picture* and the System for Identifying Motivated Abilities in *The Truth about You* ask you to look for patterns in your past activities. Skills tend to show up at an early age and continue throughout life. Because they have been with you a long time, they create patterns you can see if you know how to look for them.

Unfortunately, I know from experience that many people will not do skills analysis exercises—they simply are not that persistent with details or that linear and analytical with their thinking. That's a shame, because the skills analysis is the best and quickest tool available. However, I do have some second-best options for people who can't get through the exercises.

One technique is to ask people who know you well what they think you do best. You may be surprisingly blind to your strengths—so close to yourself that you can't see. You may think that because *you* are good at something, everyone else is too, or if a task comes easily to you, then it's no big deal. Perhaps your strongest skills come so easily and naturally that you are barely aware of using them. It may never have occurred to you that you could earn a living by doing these things you do so effortlessly.

Originally I considered counseling as a career because people kept suggesting it for me. They knew, better than I, how well I listened. Even now, it is so easy for me to listen, to empathize with other people, that sometimes I don't feel like I'm really working when I am counseling. Sometimes I even feel as though I should be trying harder, putting forth the same kind of effort that I would if I was, say, scrubbing the floor. It shouldn't come so easily, whispers the Puritan in me. It should feel like work in the most negative sense of the word.

Here are some questions to ask yourself:

- **Question #1:** What are you doing when you are so engrossed or absorbed or involved that you lose track of time? Brainstorm, write the activities down or tell them to a friend who writes them down, and then look for themes or patterns. What do the activities have in common? One client found that he was happiest and most absorbed when he was collecting and organizing things—from beer cans to butterflies. Archiving was a natural career choice for him.

• **Question #2:** In what kinds of activities, relative to yourself and not others, do you make the boldest choices and take the greatest risks? Very likely it is in those areas where you have the most intuitive confidence in yourself. Again, brainstorm, write your activities down, and look for themes or patterns in your answers. One of my friends was most avant garde with her clothing. She took risks and dressed unlike anybody else, and seemed to have a knack for staying one step ahead of fashion. After modeling for a couple years she began to design clothing.

• **Question #3:** What are your occupational daydreams? Think about all the work-related daydreams you've ever had, even when you were a kid. Look for themes and for the kinds of work you imagined yourself doing. Take them seriously. One client confessed that he had always dreamed of running off to join the circus and had many fantasies of himself entertaining: juggling, clowning, riding bareback, walking the high wire. This was very hard for him to admit or act on, because his family disapproved of any kind of behavior that they interpreted as "showing off."

• **Question #4:** Another question to consider is how quickly you do certain tasks. Think of your skill in terms of running a race: anyone can cover the distance eventually, but the winner does it the quickest. Those areas where you work the most quickly, relative to others, are likely to be areas where you are more skilled. To use myself as an example again, I am very fast when it comes to using words. I spoke in sentences early for my age and read quickly once I learned how. I can remember friends watching me read in junior high and exclaiming at how fast my eyes were moving! Now almost all my work involves words—reading, writing, speaking, or listening to them.

On the other hand, my finger dexterity is only in the 15th percentile, meaning that if 100 people took a finger dexterity race (putting pegs in a pegboard), 85 of them would finish ahead of me. When I told my sister about my low score, she laughed and said she remembered that when we were kids and she asked me to cut her hair, I stood behind her breathing nervously and cutting slowly.

I mention both my strengths and weaknesses because we all have them. People are as different from each other in their skills as they are in their appearance. Areas of low aptitude can actually be helpful, in that they help you decide what you *don't* want to do. And, although we might feel prejudice against people whose abilities do not mirror our own, it's just as legitimate to be bad as to be good at something.

Of course, you'll do things more quickly with practice—it's not all aptitude. But people tend to prefer those areas where they have more aptitude and over time will attain greater skill and speed performing related tasks, as compared to people who are not so naturally gifted. For example, even though I have had plenty of practice cooking, I don't really enjoy it, and I am amazed at how fast chefs work. Working with food and kitchen utensils, I am slow and tense and eager to be done with it—perhaps because I legitimately fear that I'm about to chop off a finger. My artist sister, on the other hand, says she finds working with her hands relaxing. Even though she is working meticulously and precisely, she is relaxed and at ease. She has considered such careers as teaching art, illustrating children's books, and painting forgeries (copies of well-known works), none of which would suit me.

If you do a skills analysis exercise, you will get immediate feedback on your preferred skills. But if you ask yourself the above questions about what you do quickly and daringly and when you lose track of time, don't expect your first answers to be the final answers. Be alert to patterns that emerge as you remember your past, become more aware of your present behavior, and dream of what you'd like to do in the future. Your skills will gradually become clearer, as though you were focusing a camera lens.

"Contentment comes from identifying the gifts you have been given, submitting them to the necessary training, and then engaging them in work."

—Arthur F. Miller

The Forest of Creative Occupations

Imagine that you stand before a Forest of Creative Occupations. You will enter this forest in a spirit of exploration, looking at occupations that will allow you to take a creative role. You are in the Artistic corner of the work world, the region with the least structure and the greatest opportunity to do something new and different. There will be a variety of occupations here that suit you.

57

More than anything else, this forest is a place where people work with ideas. Instead of the routine and concrete work that characterizes the other worlds of work, here you find creative and abstract occupations that require you to become very involved with information, and to bring information together in new products or services. (Compared to work in the other five corners of the hexagon, Artistic work requires among the highest aptitudes for color discrimination, finger dexterity, spatial ability, and intelligence.) This forest is vital, alive, growing. New trees are springing up and the whole forest is expanding.

As America moves out of the Industrial Age and into the Information Age, the soil under our feet is changing. Intangible ideas are taking root as we move from an economy based on the production of goods to an economy based on the provision of services. The number of blue-collar workers—those who labor mostly with their bodies—is growing smaller, replaced by an ever-increasing group of white-collar workers, laboring mostly with their brains. By the year 2000 it is predicted that 80 percent of jobs in the U.S. will require brainpower rather than brawn.

"Empires of the future are empires of the mind."

—WINSTON CHURCHILL

Futurists tell us that tomorrow's economy will reward people who can work symbolically with information. In *Powershift*,[20] Alvin Toffler argues that knowledge—not land, raw materials, labor, or capital—is the primary resource and base for a new world economy. Data, information, and knowledge will be key, and those who can work with them will be in demand. More and more, he believes, our culture is becoming dependent on the manipulation of symbols. "At every step from today, it is knowledge, not cheap labor; symbols, not raw materials, that embody and add value."

In *The Work of Nations*,[21] Secretary of Labor Robert Reich describes the emergence of three broad categories of work. The first two categories he calls **routine production services** (e.g., blue-collar work or data processing) and **in-person services** (e.g., retail sales work and waiting

tables.) Both of these broad categories of services involve relatively simple and repetitive tasks that offer little for the creative person. In these
kinds of jobs, your wages depend on the amount of time you have worked
or the amount of work you have done. It is very likely that you have a
supervisor and unlikely that you would do the work at all if you weren't
getting paid.

The third category Reich dubs **symbolic-analytic services.** It
involves creating patterns in abstract information by manipulating symbols, such as numbers, words, and pictures, and includes engineering and
consulting—and many kinds of Artistic work! For this kind of work, your
income is not directly related to the amount of time you spend at work
or how much you have produced. Instead it is more directly related to
how clever you are with ideas, and how much of a world market there is
for those ideas. Rather than having a boss, you probably work alone or
with a small group of associates. Rather than repeating the same concrete
task over and over, most of your time is spent finding and solving new
problems. Because this kind of work is more intrinsically motivating, you
might very well want to do it even if you weren't getting paid.

For many creative and unconventional people, this kind of symbolic
work with ideas is precisely their cup of tea. They like reshaping goods
and services in new and magical ways that enhance their usefulness or
delightfulness. If present trends continue and the futurists are right, it will
be the dawning of an age of opportunity for Artistic types.

If you'd like to move into the symbolic-analytic services sector, look
for ways that you can **add value to information in the service of
others**. There are lots of ways to do this, from conducting the
Philharmonic to designing a new landscape that enhances already existing structures. Adding new information to old information adds value, if
it's done in a way that improves what previously existed. Products become
better products by the addition of ideas in the form of advanced technology and knowledge. Let's look at some examples.

With the movie *Beauty and the Beast*, the creative people at Walt
Disney Studios took a well-known story (the "information" in this case)
and added value to it in many different ways. Writers developed the story
and wrote a screenplay; cartoonists created and animated characters; actors
and actresses provided voices; artists designed backgrounds and special

59

effects and computer-generated imagery; composers and lyricists wrote an original score; instrumental musicians and singers performed the songs; directors and editors brought it all together into a pleasing whole.

Creative and unconventional people can add value in other ways as well. As a counselor, I add value to the information my clients give me, by providing a different perspective, making connections outside their awareness, or validating and normalizing their experience. My brother-in-law, a self-employed economist, adds value to an unwieldy mass of public data provided by the government. By selecting the most relevant data, analyzing it with appropriate software and organizing it according to economic principles, he puts economic information into a usable form that is tailored to the unique needs of each of his clients.

In the Forest of Creative Occupations, you'll find many ways to serve others by working symbolically with information. Your challenge is to find ways to use your gifts to solve someone else's problems (and their "problem" could simply be getting more enjoyment or enrichment from life).

Back to Skills Again

Your favorite skills can help you orient yourself in the forest. The U.S. Department of Labor analyzes occupations in three major skills categories: 1) skills with ideas (or information or data), 2) skills with people, and 3) skills with things. The results of your formal skills analysis are already organized in this way. If you haven't done the formal analysis but you did ask yourself the earlier questions about skills (on pages 54–55), take a look at your answers and see if your skills fall mostly into the ideas, people, or things categories.

If you are unsure, ask yourself how **involved** you want to be with ideas, people, and things. Or, to rephrase it, you could ask how **intimately** you want to work with **ideas** or **people** or **things**. If you still don't know, begin with those categories where you have the greatest patience. Or, conversely, avoid those that require you to deal with whatever you find the most exasperating, such as difficult people or things that don't work.

One of my clients orginally thought that she wanted to teach French, an occupation that involves both ideas and people. However, after teaching junior high for awhile, she found that she was too thin-skinned and sensitive, easily upset when students were rude or disinterested. After taking a closer look at her skills and what she was doing when she lost track of time, she realized that what she really wanted was to work more intimately with ideas and things and less intimately with people. She had a flair for design and liked to work with computers, and without getting further training she is now happily employed as a computer artist.

Keep in mind that you don't need to restrict yourself to just ideas *or* people *or* things. You could very well want to do two or more kinds of work, each drawing on different combinations of skills. In my case, I want to work with ideas almost all the time, and people about half the time. Writing lets me work almost exclusively with ideas, and counseling lets me become intimately involved with both ideas and people. On the other hand, because I don't want to work with things more than I have to, I won't even look in that direction for a career.

Now let's take a look at the entire forest and the four main trails leading into it. Because we are in an idea forest, each trail involves ideas (or information, or data) to some degree. You can go down the path that involves ideas almost exclusively, or the path that involves ideas *and* people, or the path that involves ideas *and* things, or the path that involves ideas *and* people *and* things. Each path leads to different occupational trees that have in common the higher-level skills required to do that kind of work.

61

The Four Trails

1. Idea Trail

Writers

Directors

Performers

Investigators

Coordinator

Evaluators

Promoters

Organizers

If these types of jobs interest you, skip to Trail 1, page 63.

2. Ideas and People Trail

Mentors

Negotiators

Instructors

Supervisors

Persuaders

If these types of jobs interest you, skip to Trail 2, page 66.

3. Ideas and Things Trail

Designers

Image Makers

Photographers

Performers

Electronic Designers

Finishers

Model Builders

Food Preparers

Restorers

If these types of jobs interest you, skip to Trail 3, page 68.

4. Ideas and People and Things Trail

Teachers

Supervisors

Entertainers

Caregivers

Models

If these types of jobs interest you, skip to Trail 4, page 72.

You want to move through the whole forest to the parts that appeal most to you. So let's take a closer look at the four different parts of the forest. In each of the four areas you will find a listing of primary skills, followed by several specific occupations that require those skills, along with their Holland codes and page numbers. Once you've found individual occupations that sound interesting to you, turn to the back of the book for more information. There you will find a description of each occupation in the Career Reference Section, as well as a discussion of the types of employers who might hire you to do that kind of work.

This Career Reference Section contains all the still-viable occupations listed in the latest *Dictionary of Occupational Titles* (1991 at this writing) that had an A in either the first or second place of their Holland code, meaning that they are classified as primarily or secondarily Artistic in nature. In addition, you will find some brand new careers not yet listed in the *DOT* including some which I added based on conversations with Gary Gottfredson and my reading of more recent publications.[22]

63

TRAIL 1: IDEAS

Here we find jobs that require a high degree of involvement with intangible ideas and lesser involvement with people or things. I will further divide this group approximately in half, separating out those occupations that permit the greatest creativity. These are the occupations that require synthesizing or integrating ideas.

The occupations allowing for the greatest creativity are further divided according to skills used on the job. Here we have writers of all kinds, including writers of music; directors, who bring together the creative work of others; performers; and investigators.

IDEAS: ALLOW THE GREATEST CREATIVITY

Writers

Arranger AEI

Biographer ASE

Columnist/Commentator EAS

Composer ASE

Continuity Writer AES

Copywriter ASI

Critic AES

Crossword-Puzzle Maker ASE

Editorial Writer AES

Humorist ASE

Librettist ASE

Lyricist ASE

Orchestrator AEI

Playwright ASE

Poet AES

Reader AES

Reporter★ ASI

Screenwriter AEI

Writer, Prose, Fiction and
  Nonfiction AIE

Directors

Artist and Repertoire Manager★
  AES

Bureau Chief AES

Choral Director AES

Creative Director AES

Conductor, Orchestra AES

Director, Music AES

Director, Stage AES

Editor, Book AES

Editor, Greeting Card AES

Editor, News AES

Performers

Actor AES

Clown EAC

Comedian AES

Dancer AER

Impersonator AES

Mime AEI

Singer AES

Ventriloquist AES

Investigators

Biologist★★ IAR

Economist IAS

Experimental Psychologist★★
  IAE

Social Psychologist IAE

★ May allow for less creativity
★★ May also work intimately with things

The remaining ideas occupations fall into these categories: coordinators, who direct a sequence of activities, most often the work of others, and sometimes with the purpose of developing better information; evaluators; promoters; and organizers of collections. While at first glance it may be hard to conceive of some of these jobs as creative, they are included because they involve problem solving, and people who can analyze and present information in new and unconventional ways will do well in these fields.

IDEAS: ALLOW LESS CREATIVITY

65

Coordinators

Account Executive AES

Contestant Coordinator AES

Department Head, College
or University EAI

Director of Vital Statistics EAI

Director, Classification and
Treatment AES

Director, Instructional
Material ASE

Director, Program AES

Director, State-Assessed
Properties AEI

Location Manager EAR

Manager, Forms Analysis EAS

Manager, Records Analysis EAI

Manager, Reports Analysis EAS

Music Supervisor EAS

Program Coordinator AES

Sight-Effects Specialist AES

Traffic-Safety Administrator AER

IDEAS: ALLOW LESS CREATIVITY

Evaluators

Appraiser, Art IAS

Bar Examiner AES

Cryptanalyst AIE

Field Representative EAS

Graphologist ACS

Intelligence Research Specialist AEI

Intelligence Specialist AES

Patent Agent AEI

Promoters

Auctioneer AES

Fashion Coordinator EAS

Public-Relations Representative★ EAS

Sales-Service Promoter AES

Collections Organizers

Acquisitions Librarian SAI

Archivist AES

Audiovisual Librarian EAS

Young-Adult Librarian AES

TRAIL 2: IDEAS AND PEOPLE

The occupations that require working intimately with ideas and people are organized by the skills used with people: mentors, who guide people, often following established principles in their field; negotiators, who solve problems by exchanging ideas with others; instructors; supervisors; and persuaders.

★Allows greater creativity

IDEAS AND PEOPLE

Mentors

Clergy Member SAE

Counselor SAE

Dance Therapist ASI

Marriage and Family Therapist SAE

Music Therapist ASI

Speech Pathologist SAI

67

Negotiators

Commissioner, Conservation of Resources AES

Director, Council on Aging EAS

Editor, Newspaper★ AES

Editor, Technical and Scientific Publications★ ASE

Supervisor, Historic Sites AES

Instructors

Cantor★ ASE

Choreographer AES

Dramatic Coach★ ASE

Graduate Assistant SAE

Instructor, Dancing★ ASE

Instructor, Modeling ASE

Liberal Arts Faculty SAI

Librarian SAI

Teacher, Drama★ ASE

Teacher, Elementary School SAI

Teacher, Preschool SAE

Teacher, Secondary School SAE

Trainer SAE

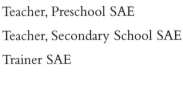

★Allows greater creativity

IDEAS AND PEOPLE

Supervisors	**Persuaders**
Editor, City★ AES	Sales Rep, Independent EAS or AES
Editor, Department AES	
Editor, Publications AES	Salesperson, Retail EAS or EAR
Production Manager, Advertising ASE	Wedding Consultant AES
Story Editor★ ASE	
Supervisor, Show Operations ASE	
Supervisor, Sign Shop EAS	

TRAIL 3: IDEAS AND THINGS

The ideas and things category is the largest. Once again, I'll separate those occupations that allow for the greatest creativity. They fall into these categories: designers, who select and balance tangible elements for a particular purpose; image makers, who often work with fewer media and whose purpose may primarily be an esthetic response; photographers; and performers.

IDEAS AND THINGS: ALLOW GREATER CREATIVITY

Designers

Architect AIR

Art Director AES

Bank-Note Designer AER

Cloth Designer AER

Clothes Designer ASR

Color Expert AES

Commercial Designer AER

Display Designer AES

★Allows greater creativity

Designers

Displayer, Merchandise ARE

Exhibit Designer ASE

Floral Designer RAE

Fur Designer ACS

Furniture Designer AES

Graphic Designer AER

Industrial Designer AES

Interior Designer ASE

Landscape Architect AIR

Memorial Designer AER

Package Designer AEI

Safety-Clothing-and-Equipment
   Developer AER

Set Decorator AES

Set Designer, Motion Picture AIE

Set Designer, Theater AES

69

Image-Makers

Bonsai Culturist★ RAE

Cartoonist AES

Cartoonist, Motion Pictures
   AES

Fashion Artist AEI

Illustrator AER

Illustrator, Medical and
   Scientific AIE

Illustrator, Set AES

Make-Up Artist AER

Painter ASI

Pewterer ARS

Police Artist ASC

Printmaker AES

Quick Sketch Artist ASE

Sculptor AER

Silhouette Artist AES

Stained-Glass Artist ASE

★May allow for less creativity

IDEAS AND THINGS: ALLOW GREATER CREATIVITY

Photographers

Camera Operator AES

Director of Photography AES

Photographer, Still ARS

Photojournalist AEC

Performers

Laserist ASI

Magician AES

Musician, Instrumental ASI

Puppeteer AEI

The remaining ideas and things occupations are: electronic designers, who produce something visual on computers and television screens; finishers, who complete a project that was designed or originated by someone else; model builders; food preparers; and restorers.

IDEAS AND THINGS: ALLOW LESS CREATIVITY

Electronic Designers

Computer Artist ASE

Film or Videotape Editor AES

Media Production Specialist★ AES

Program Director, Cable Television EAS

Programmer-Analyst IAC

Television Technician★ ASI

Finishers

Artist, Suspect ASE

Body-Make-Up Artist AER

Copyist AES

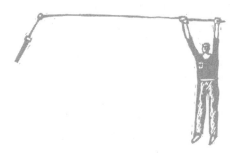

★Allows greater creativity

Finishers

Crafter, Jewelry ARE

Decorator, Mannequin RAE

Engrosser ARE

Exhibit Artist ASI

Instructor, Painting AES

Milliner AES

Optical-Effects Camera
Operator ARS

Optical-Effects Layout
Person ASC

Painter, Hand ARE

Pewter Finisher RAS

Sound-Effects Technician RAE

Stone Carver RAE

Tattoo Artist AEC

Wallcovering Texturer ASR

Model Builders

Concrete Sculptor RAI

Exhibit Builder ARS

Glass Blower, Laboratory
Apparatus RAE

Modeler, Brick and Tile★ ARI

Model Maker, Pottery and
Porcelain RAE

Model Maker ARI

Miniature-Set Constructor ARE

Stage Technician ARS

Food Preparers

Cake Decorator ARE

Chef de Froid RAE

Cook, Pastry RAS

Decorator, Dairy Products AES

Ice Cream Chef RAS

Restorers:

Musical Instrument Repairer
RAS/E

Paintings Conservator ASR

Restorer, Ceramic ASI

Restorer, Paper-and-Prints AIS

71

★Allows greater creativity

TRAIL 4: IDEAS AND PEOPLE AND THINGS

The final category is a bit of a hodge-podge in which skills with ideas and people and things are roughly equivalent. Included here are teachers, supervisors, entertainers, care-givers, and models. Once again, some of these jobs may not seem particularly creative, but research shows that creative people are attracted to them, often because they allow some freedom and flexibility.

IDEAS AND PEOPLE AND THINGS

Teachers

Teacher, Art★ ASE

Teacher, Music AES

Supervisors

Art Director★ AES

Inspector, Screen Printing ASR

Manager, Display★ AES

Pastry Chef ASE

Supervisor, Suspect Artist ASE

Supervisor, Scenic Arts AES

Entertainers

Acrobat AER

Amusement Park Entertainer AES

Double AER

Equestrian AER

Impersonator, Character EAS

Psychic Reader AEC

Ring Conductor EAS

Singing Messenger ASC

Wire Walker AER

Care-Givers

Child Care Attendant SAI

Models

Model EAS

Model, Artists' AES

Model, Photographer's AES

★Allows greater creativity

Now What?

Now that you've got an overview, go to the Career Reference Section at the back of the book and wander through your favorite part of the forest. Or you could just go straight to those occupations that most appeal to you. Occupations have been organized by skill, increasing the chance that you will recognize those skills you have and most enjoy using when you see them all together. Once you have considered many different options, narrow down so that you have at least two job titles to research but less than ten.

If your skill area leaves you with too many options, all of which are appealing, try Dr. Caela Farren's good idea and focus on your preferred field. Fields cut across the ideas-people-things structure, and are more stable than job titles. Possible fields include education, advertising, music, fashion, psychology, etc. So, for example, if advertising is your field and you know you want roughly equal involvement with ideas and people and information, then you could look into becoming an art director.

Another way to narrow down is to use your Holland code. You don't need to find an exact match with your three-letter code, but you might eliminate from further consideration those that don't provide a good overlap. If your code is AIR, for example, then SAE occupations would probably not be close enough, but IAR or RAI or even AIC occupations would be worth looking into.

A different way to narrow down is to think about the kinds of ideas or people or things you like to work with. For example, you could work with ideas about art history, individual differences, or agricultural economics. In the people category you could work with preschoolers or dancers or prisoners. In the things category you could work with museum exhibits or cameras or puppets. There is an infinite variety of possibilities, and you can pick your favorites.

A way to narrow down and open up at the same time is to consider different ways to do the same job. If you'd like to play music, for example, you could do that in the music hall, on the street, in a cozy restaurant, or just for yourself and your friends. If you'd like to teach, you can teach any age group, in businesses and retirement centers as well as grade schools and colleges. If you'd like to design, you could design in two dimensions—from postage stamp size to billboard size—or in three dimensions, from earring size to space station size.

Once you have narrowed down to several possibilities, you need to gather information about each one before you can make any final decisions. A good place to start is the public library. Give the career librarian your job titles and ask for help locating more information. When you have learned as much as you can through printed or computer sources, talk to people who do that kind of work. If you are still interested, a great way to learn more is through professional associations and work experience as a volunteer or intern. In certain fields, you will learn that you need to get some training before you can begin.

Even if you are really excited about only one option, keep a first alternate in mind. Sometimes things don't work out as you had hoped, and it truly helps your peace of mind to know that you have attractive alternatives. In my own case, my current career is a Plan C. It helped to know it was there when I saw All the Problems I Could Not Overcome with Plan B. (Plan B was to create programming for cable television, which I discovered required me to be too Enterprising and also required too much involvement with things and not enough involvement with people.)

As you seek information on your most attractive options, be prepared for some frustration. My major source of information for the Artistic occupations described in the Career Reference Section was the *Dictionary of Occupational Titles*.[23] While it is the best resource of its kind, it is sadly out of date. Some very quaint and old-fashioned occupations are still listed, and some exciting new occupations haven't yet been added. People are working right now to update the *Dictionary* and bring it online, but I've been told that the new and improved version won't be ready until the end of the '90s, at the earliest.

Remember that the Forest of Creative Occupations is evolving, with some grand old trees dying out and some new trees just springing up on the forest floor, barely noticeable and not yet named. If you'd like to anticipate emerging growth areas, look for opportunities to create something new with information, especially if it appeals to the senses. Some areas that seem promising to me are designing and programming multimedia software, planning and implementing educational vacations and leisure activities, and negotiating or promoting intellectual property.

Now, let's consider the advantages and disadvantages of using job titles. The nice thing about using job titles is that people like them. They are so definite and graspable that they lend security to both speaker and listener. Job titles can be useful little symbols that save you a paragraph of job description. When you are doing your own investigation into the work that appeals to you most, it's helpful to know what people in the field call themselves, so you can make a better first impression by speaking their language.

The problem with job titles is that the world of work is very fluid. Organizing information by job titles, as I have done here, gives you the impression that different occupations are crisp and neat and non-overlapping. However, as you will quickly learn, that is just not true. Let me give you some examples. There are few people earning a living as full-time color experts, but there *are* many graphic designers or interior designers who do the work of a color expert as part of their jobs. There are few bona-fide fashion coordinators, but a variety of sales promoters in the fashion industry do some fashion coordination.

On the other hand, some occupations not listed here combine the work of a number of occupations already described. An independent filmmaker, for example, does the work of a scriptwriter, set designer, camera operator, director, editor—and sometimes even actor! Instructional design, an occupation not yet listed in the *DOT,* can include some of the work done by trainers, graphic designers, computer artists, media production specialists, and instructional material directors.

The point is to use job titles when they help you but to keep your attention on the kinds of work you want to do. The ways we label and categorize work are more changeable than the skills required. The most important point is to not let yourself get boxed in by a rigid job title. Try to use the labels as a springboard to expanded possibility. Once you have enough information, you can flexibly "compose" your own favorite work choices into a career. The elements of your composition will be the kinds of creative work you want to do and the ways you want to put them together. (More about that in the next chapter.)

Things are changing so fast that all printed resources, including this one, are at least a little out of date. After you've done your background research, the best way to get current information about the work that interests you is to talk to people who do that kind of work right now. If you would like some help, follow the advice in Howard Figler's *The Complete Job-Search Handbook*[24] or *What Color Is Your Parachute?*, especially the PIE interviewing strategy. Both books can also help you with the process of how to get a job, once you've decided which job you want.

If None of These Are for You

If you have looked over the 200-plus creative occupations listed in the Career Reference Section, and none of them please you, here are some suggestions.

Don't expect to be hit by a thunderbolt. I have never once seen a career client go into ecstasy over an option we turned up during counseling. Only once did a young man literally hurry out the door because he was so excited that he couldn't wait to begin. If anything, people seem more likely to resist their best and most natural choices.

Go back to chapters 1 and 2 and read or re-read them. The better you understand your gifts, the better able you will be to find ways to match your gifts to the needs of the marketplace. If you didn't do the skills analysis before, consider doing it now.

Order a specimen kit of the Self-Directed Search from Psychological Assessment Resources (PAR), 800-331-TEST. Fill out the Assessment Booklet, then look through the Occupations Finder that comes with it for all possible combinations of your three letter Holland Code. You may find occupations with an A as the *third* letter of their Holland codes, such as hair stylist or interpreter, that appeal to you. Then go to the reference desk at your library, ask for the *Dictionary of Occupational Titles*, and read the description of what a worker does in those jobs. (The Career Reference section at the back of this book only include jobs with A as the first or second letter.)

Maybe for you, **how** you work will be more important than what you do. You may be the kind of person who can do more conventional work but still express an artistic style. As Fred Astaire said, even a garbage can can be picked up artistically.

Adapt an occupation that appeals to you somewhat. For example, if you like the idea of becoming a dance or music therapist, but dance and music are not your strength, you could become an art therapist or psychodramatist. Or maybe instead of conserving paintings, you'd like to conserve architecture or textiles or sculpture. Remember, Quentin Tarantino, one of today's hottest movie directors, got his start working in a video store—and turned what most people would consider a dead-end job into an educational opportunity.

Conduct your own investigation into possible creative work that is so new or rare that it is not described in the usual sources. The jobs listed above are only the most traditional Artistic occupations. There are many more possibilities, but you will have to work harder to find them. For example, food stylist is an example of an occupation not listed in the *DOT*. Food stylists arrange food aesthetically, so that photographers can take the pictures that appear in cookbooks. With a little diligent investigation, you can discover additional possibilities.

You could even create your own unconventional job—something that has never been done before, or a combination of existing jobs that is uniquely yours. For more on this, see the next chapter.

77

"I feel more confident and more satisfied when I reflect that I have two professions and not one. Medicine is my lawful wife and literature is my mistress. When I get tired of one I spend the night with the other. Though it's disorderly it's not so dull, and besides, neither really loses anything through my infidelity."

—ANTON CHEKHOV

Compose Your Own Career

LET'S COME OUT OF THE FOREST NOW and sit on this hill where you can arrange a composition of work activities that provides for both creative expression and financial survival. Here we will look at how you can form your career choices into a viable structure or lifestyle. As writers and musicians and artists choose esthetic elements and arrange them in an original composition, you can choose creative work along with other kinds of work and arrange them into your own unique career.

I am using the word "work" in its broadest sense, meaning *what you do with your time.* For example, your creative work could be paid work, or volunteer work, or a hobby. You could work for yourself or for others. You could go to an office or stay at home. You could work part-time and/or full-time. Your creative aspirations could be the central theme, explaining everthing else, or they could be more of an embellishment on a traditional theme.

There isn't a map for this chapter so much as there is a roster of alternate routes. Up to now, the major route was to take one salaried position and keep it for most of your life. Although this has a lot to be said for it, especially in terms of security, it is an approach that has not worked well for Holland's Artistic types.

In fact, it's not working well for almost anybody these days, because our workplace is undergoing dramatic transition. Corporations are merging and downsizing; many occupations have become obsolete; automation has taken its toll. Organizations are trimming their regular staff and hiring part-time or temporary workers and freelancers to cut down on costs. Job security is becoming a thing of the past. In fact, it is predicted that by the year 2000, full-time workers will be a minority.

The good news is that unconventional people often adapt well to a changing world. Rather than bemoaning the loss of the conventional life-time job with a single employer, we actually appreciate the freedom and flexibility provided by taking an unconventional approach. Let's start by looking at the major approaches to working with organizations. In *The Age of Unreason*[25], futurist Charles Handy describes three emerging groups of workers.

First is a core of executives and professionals who work long hard hours and are very well compensated. They are essential to the organiza-tion and their lives are dominated by it. Most of them work at jobs that are Enterprising and Conventional in nature, but many Artistic jobs that involve directing and managing the work of other people would also fall into this category. This would include such occupations as advertising executive, newspaper editor, and classification and treatment director.

The second group of workers are specialists who work on contract. Given that the results of their work matter more than the time they spend doing it, they have greater control than salaried wage earners over their working hours. Creative people who freelance their services and apply their talents to practical problems fall into this category, such as writers and graphic designers and tradeshow magicians. They may work on a freelance or contract basis for a number of different organizations. They may be paid by the hour or get a flat fee.

The third group are part-time, temporary workers who are hired when extra help is needed and let go when the job is done. These tem-porary workers are usually hired for jobs that require less skill or training than those mentioned above. People who make their creative activities a priority might work part-time in survival jobs like these, making less money but having more time for clowning or writing poetry or creating stained-glass windows. They may prefer the freedom provided by tem-porary work to the constraints that are usually part of a salaried position.

You will notice that these three groups of workers move from being more to less dependent on organizations, going from a life dominated by the organization to a life more independent of an organization. The following options I have ordered according to the degree of involvement required with an employing organization. Here are eight different options from which you can pick and choose to create your own career composition:

1) Take an Artistic job as a way to earn your living;

2) Take a non-Artistic job and make your creative activities a hobby;

3) Take a bread-and-butter job to support your creative ambitions;

4) Run a small business marketing your creative work;

5) Teach in your field;

6) Freelance in your field;

7) Get a grant or find a patron;

8) Create your own job.

You might use just one, several, or all eight routes at different times in your life. You can move fluidly from one to another as circumstances change, and you can use more than one route at a time. Maybe you'll even discover some routes that I don't know about.

Now let's look at the real-life compositions of some creative people who have followed one or more of these eight options, beginning with a story about a person whose career path is one many Artistic types might aspire to.

Career Option One: Take an Artistic Job

The most traditional approach is to take a full-time job with an employer who will pay you to do the kind of creative work you want to do. This approach has a big practical advantage—the security of daily employment and a set salary. Chapter 3 assumed that this would be your preferred strategy and listed a multitude of Artistic jobs from which to choose.

Bill Hinson is an example of a person who followed this strategy. When I interviewed Bill, he worked as a graphic designer for the public library in Memphis, Tennessee. The library provided him with a nice studio, including a camera, computer, and a couple small presses. He also taught graphic design part-time at Memphis State University. Since then he has taken a job as a graphic designer with Malcolm Greer Designers in Providence, Rhode Island.

The unusual part of Bill's story is that he didn't even try his hand at art until he was forty-three. Just before he entered art school he ended his career in marketing because it was not a good fit and he was unhappy with corporate life. "I've always been partial to the visual in my environment," says Bill, a closet doodler all his life. Though he had no confidence for art school, he applied to and was admitted to the Rhode Island School of Design.

The next three years he lived away from his family, two children aged eighteen and seven, and a supportive wife with a good job at Federal Express. Times were tight financially and he worried about his family back home and about how he would get into a new career at his age, but he found joy in the work and developed great friendships with artists from all over the world. "I got my first degree for my parents," he said. "Twenty years later, I got an M.F.A. for myself."

Bill believes that people need to feel passionate about their career direction. His advice for people with aspirations similar to his own? "Get started. Take the first step. Start locally, gain some experience and confidence, and then see what you want to do next." His advice for himself at seventeen (and others like him): "Don't be afraid to defy the norm. If you search honestly, you will make the right decisions for yourself."

Career Option 2: Have a Non-Artistic Job and a Creative Hobby

One way to arrange your work is to take a non–Artistic job and develop one or more creative hobbies. Sometimes hobbies turn into careers, but then again, some hobbyists would never want their personal fun to turn into work that they do for someone else.

Joyce Tsuji is a biologist turned environmental toxicologist. She enjoys her work for a consulting firm and she also enjoys her hobbies. Two of her hobbies—karate and bonsai—reflect her Japanese heritage. Joyce notes that bonsai reflects Asian culture: "In bonsai, a young tree is not worth much. The experience and character of a tree add value."

Joyce buys crooked, ugly orphan trees from a nursery or starter trees from a bonsai nursery and trims the roots to create dwarfed trees, pruning and shaping the branches to make them look old. Each of Joyce's twenty-five trees is markedly different—reflecting her sensitivity to the uniqueness not just of each tree, but of all plants and animals.

Five years ago, Joyce and her husband took a bonsai class and now practice bonsai together, finding it a bit like watching children grow. She finds bonsai to be a spiritual activity, a process she enjoys for the journey, not the end. Some of her trees express her vision of nature now; others won't have the effect she desires for another ten years. Although bonsai is a time commitment and something to be conscientious about, her hobby helps her to take her mind off work, stay centered, and stop more often to enjoy life in a world that seems focused on making money and achieving results.

83

When choosing a hobby, Joyce recommends that it be "different from what you do on a daily basis." She also recommends joining clubs as a way to meet people and see if you are really interested in the activity. Hobby clubs, like the bonsai club she belongs to in Seattle, offer programs and shows and ways to get started.

Career Option 3: Take a Bread-and-Butter Job

People who want to do creative work often need to work at another job until they establish themselves. A day job to support yourself works well for many people, and is especially well-suited to our current job-market. Temporary agencies can help you find such work. You might want to work part-time, gradually decreasing bread-and-butter activities as you begin to make more money on your creative endeavors.

In *The Complete Job-Search Handbook*, Howard Figler includes a chapter on interim jobs. He lists four criteria for choosing an interim job, acknowledging that its unlikely you'll find one interim job that meets all four criteria. His criteria are:

1) a large enough income for you and your dependents to live on without great stress;

2) easily obtainable work that doesn't require years of training and is thus relatively easy for you to take and to leave;

3) work that makes only moderate demands on your time so that you have time and energy left over for a job search (and/or your creative endeavors);

4) continuous exposure to a variety of people so that you can make contacts during work time and learn about new career opportunities.

Since you may keep your survival job indefinitely, I would add two other criteria. First, find survival work that fits your personality. Your personality may be mostly Artistic, and you may prefer to only do Artistic work, but your personality is not purely Artistic. You have other skills and interests that you can parlay into a job. Others have done it: For example, Wallace Stevens was a poet and vice president of an insurance company; T.S. Eliot was a poet and a bank clerk; Spinoza was a philosopher and a lens grinder. For the next couple years or the rest of your life, you may have to do non-Artistic work to put bread on the table. You don't *have* to starve in a garret. Barbara Sher recommends that you take a day job you don't hate and call it your "subsidy to the arts!"

Secondly, as poet and Jungian counselor Susan Scott says, it's important to choose work that won't interfere with your psychic life. Some work doesn't fully occupy your mind, leaving you time on the job to mull over esthetic choices. Other work leaves you so frazzled and stressed that you have trouble turning to your creative projects even when you are off the job. If you don't now know what kinds of work will or won't interfere with your psyche, you will find out through trial and error.

> *"The best time for planning a book is while*
> *you are doing the dishes."*
>
> —AGATHA CHRISTIE

A good place to start looking for your bread-and-butter work is the second or third letter of your Holland code. To help you do that, I have listed below many possible kinds of work you can do to support yourself as you pursue your creative goals.

Social

Some of the most popular survival jobs for Social types are bartender, security guard, mail carrier, orderly, and fast-food worker. More exotic

options include detective, comparison shopper, vending-machine attendant, paralegal assistant, and employment interviewer. Or, if you're willing to invest in the education, you might consider becoming a podiatrist,
occupational therapist, recreational therapist, or radiologic technologist.
These last choices may be especially good for Social and Artistic readers
who are security-minded and plan to pursue creative activities as a hobby.

If you have a Social streak in your personality, consider living-in as a
companion for an elderly person, a nanny for a young family, a home-
maker for busy professionals, or a home-health aide for someone who is
sick. Then you won't even have to pay rent. Or you could take people
into your home: become a foster parent or run a boarding house or a bed
and breakfast. One couple I know created a bed-and-breakfast of unusual charm and beauty. Their artistic flair is expressed in the way they have
furnished and decorated their home and in their presentation of breakfast, afternoon tea, and picnic baskets for their guests.

85

Enterprising

The largest category of survival work for those with Enterprising skills is
in retail sales. There are so many different things to sell—books, cars, pets,
china, music, cosmetics, art objects, hearing aids, toys, hardware, house-
wares, and so on. It's possible to sell intangibles, too, such as advertising
space or educational programs or vacation packages. If you have supervi-
sory skill and want to take advantage of two growth areas, consider
becoming a hotel manager or health service manager.

Some of the more popular jobs outside of management and retail
sales are telemarketer, manicurist, newspaper carrier, caterer helper, and
travel agent. Or you could be a dispatcher for the transportation or public service industries. If you'd like something a little more exotic, consider taking a job as a sightseeing guide, wine steward/stewardess, pool manager, or private investigator. And if you'd like a free apartment, you might
take a part-time position as an assistant apartment manager.

Investigative

There are fewer easily accessible Investigative jobs than any other kind,
perhaps because this kind of work often requires years of training. Lab

assistant is a general title for Investigative jobs in such diverse places as zoos, hospitals, universities, and research laboratories. Exotic possibilities include robot technician; medical lab technician; chemical preparer (compounding chemical ingredients and performing standard tests); touch-up painter (covering scratches, chips, and repairs on the painted finish of appliances and cars); line-service attendant (servicing aircraft before flight); and phlebotomist (drawing blood).

If you have a strong Investigative streak to your personality and plan to pursue creative activities as a hobby, you might consider getting the training required for a mainstream Investigative job such as a registered nurse, engineer, optometrist, physical or respiratory therapist, physician assistant, or medical technologist. You're likely to be well compensated for your time and to be able to leave work behind at the end of the day.

Realistic

Bread-and-butter work abounds for Artistic types who also have Realistic skills and interests. Some popular interim jobs include janitor, house-cleaner, bus driver, taxi driver, truck driver, and horticultural worker. More exotic opportunities include masseur/masseuse, fireworks maker, computer service technician, dog and cat food cook, and cremator. General job titles with almost infinite variations are cleaner, painter, repairer, cook, machine operator, fisher, and laborer.

If it would further your Artistic goals to not have to pay rent and you like the country, you might look for a job as a live-in laborer on a farm or ranch. If you'd like a place to live in the city, perhaps you could become a chauffeur or caretaker. If you would rather be more independent and still earn a decent wage, you might learn a skilled trade—such as that of a carpenter, electrician, plumber, or paper hanger—through a vocational school or apprenticeship. Although such training will take you away from your Artistic hobby now, it may better help you support your dependents and your Artistic goals later.

Conventional

The most popular survival jobs for those with some Conventional in their personality are waiter/waitress, clerk, cashier, telephone operator,

and office temporary worker. Office temps often do the work of a secretary, receptionist, or word processor—any of which could also be done as
a Conventional survival job—but with greater flexibility and less commitment.

More unusual choices that are still Conventional in nature include
library assistant, museum attendant, meter reader, toll collector, dog
bather, and groundskeeper. Growth is expected to be very good for the
following Conventional jobs that require more training: computer-
peripheral-equipment operator, legal secretary, and medical record
technician.

87

Therese McLaughlin is a New York City actress who has supported
herself through a variety of bread-and-butter work. Primarily a stage
character actress, Therese performs in theaters in and out of New York
City, in showcases, for kids' parties, on TV soap operas, and in live-action
stunt shows. She draws on her sensitivity to human behavior to bring out
her characters' idiosyncrasies. Says Therese, "I've always been a watcher
of other people. I observe people constantly."

She moved to New York right after college and went through four
waitressing jobs in the first two weeks. She hated waitressing, and so
moved on to other ways of supporting her acting: selling stereo equipment and art deco jewelry, demonstrating microwave ovens in malls,
handing out flyers for shows, supervising housekeeping for a hotel to the
stars, and occasionally working as an office temporary. Through it all she
managed to squeeze in performing.

For the last several years Therese has supported herself by teaching
aerobics. She returned to school to become certified as an aerobics
instructor, and now she makes more money in less time, using the extra
flexibility in her schedule for auditions and shows. Because she is fit and
athletic, she is often hired to do light stunt work as well.

Among the downsides to her path, Therese lists exhaustion and inse-
curity. It's hard to maintain relationships and get home for the holidays
while balancing two full careers. "The upside," she says, "is having a hoot!"
As others her age quit theater to start families, she sees herself becoming
more employable as she gets older. Her advice to people who need to support their talent through non-Artistic work? "First, don't panic. Second,

don't let anybody ever tell you that you can't do it. Take an honest account of who and where you are and then set about doing what you need to do."

Career Option 4: Run a Small Business Marketing Your Work

If you'd like to be self-employed and you have a creative product you can sell, you could run a small business marketing your work. For example, if you design and make children's clothes, you could sell them at crafts fairs or flea markets. You could run a small shop selling flowers and your innovative floral arrangements. Or you could make one-of-a-kind hats and sell them to retail stores. Consider selling by mail order if you feel uncomfortable with face-to-face marketing.

Ken Logsdon created Post-a-Quote, a line of "correspondence cards for the literate." He selects a quote that he handwrites on a plain paneled folder, matching it with an appropriate stamp image. He hires a helper to glue the image to the folder and to package, seal, and mail the cards to stores that sell high-end greeting cards. He now has 200 accounts serviced by reps who like his work, and he tailors cards for art galleries, museums, and specialized shops, such as New Age or gay/lesbian bookstores. A quote collector and self-proclaimed literary snob, he says, "I have always lived on the words of others."

Though Ken may always have lived on the words of others, he did not always live on his card business. A self-employed insurance adjuster for twenty years, he began creating cards as a part-time lark. When a friend suggested his quit his job to make cards full time, he answered, "Do you think I'm crazy?" But as his card business picked up and Ken grew disenchanted with the insurance business, he quit his insurance job in Denver and moved to Columbia, Missouri.

He and his wife and their two children sold their large, wonderful house that was also a great financial burden and used the equity to buy down their house payment in the Midwest. Though the card business is phenomenal, it won't support a family of four without his wife's salary as a registered nurse. They don't travel as much as they used to, but no one feels deprived and no one has regrets. Although Ken now works more hours for less income, he finds his new life very satisfying.

Ken points out that he did not plan his career. He first began making cards when a friend he met at an arts fair gave him a packet of blank note cards adorned with a Churchill postage stamp. He added quotes, and, much to his surprise, sold 150 cards the first time he took them to the Tattered Cover, a Denver bookstore. Sales grew over time in a kind of chain reaction as reps contacted him, established accounts, and gave accounts to sub-reps.

Ken summarizes the main advantage and disadvantage to his path in one phrase: "Your time is your own." His advice? "Go for it. If you are competent and confident you can swim, don't be timid to dive off the high dive."

Career Option 5: Teach in Your Field

Teaching in your field is a bit like freelancing a personal service. You can teach part-time at local colleges, teach extension classes in rented space, or teach in your own home. It's a flexible self-employment option for those who don't have salaried teaching positions or who prefer to work for themselves.

Charlotte Sonne is a professional singer and private voice teacher who has successfully blended the two careers. She has had a career as a professional singer in opera, oratorio, and recital, performing as a church soloist, as a guest artist at a local university, and as a member of the Mendelssohn Choir. She considers private teaching to be a financially and emotionally rewarding part of her music career.

Charlotte teaches voice in her living room. In an average week she teaches twenty to twenty-five hour-long sessions to students who vary tremendously in age and ability. Her sensitivity to beautiful sounds helps her to pinpoint areas where her students need attention.

Charlotte's career as a self-employed voice teacher began when she was twenty-four. She performed, took private students, taught voice part-time in several colleges, and worked as a secretary between music jobs. Although she won a Metropolitan Opera audition for the state of Arizona and had a chance to make music her whole life, Charlotte wanted a family and kept her career small while her children were small. Over time, her identity has shifted from being a singer who also teaches to being a teacher who also sings. "I love both singing and teaching," says Charlotte. "My singing career is winding down, but I believe I'll teach forever."

Among the disadvantages to working at home, she says, are a lack of benefits (such as health insurance or pensions), difficulty getting away from her work, and the fact that her lessons sometimes interfere with the rest of the household's activities. Among the advantages to teaching at home are variety, flexible time, saving money on transportation and clothing, and the happiness that comes from helping people.

Charlotte's clientele, which has provided her with a stable income for ten years, was built up slowly and entirely by word of mouth. For those who would like to follow her path, she advises maintaining your fitness as a singer, keeping current with the musical profession, staying in touch with colleagues, and learning how to respond when a potential student says, "I've always wanted to sing."

Career Option 6: Do Freelance Work in Your Field

Another way to support yourself is to freelance. You can be your own boss and structure your own time, but you'll also need to market yourself and live with a less secure income. Illustrators, writers, editors, graphic designers, interior designers, and counselors commonly operate on a freelance basis. Writer's Digest Books and North Light Books sell "how-to-do-it" guides, including *Writer's Market* and *Artist's Market*, for those who would like to freelance their creative work. To get a free catalog, call 800-289-0963.

Scott Dailey is a freelance copywriter who has been self-employed for ten years. He conceives and writes advertisements, newsletters, and employee training materials for businesses in the San Francisco Bay Area. In his spare time, he is writing the music, lyrics, and script for his first musical play. For both these creative endeavors, Scott relies on his sensitivity to the sounds and rhythms of music and language.

Because as a young writer he had scorned advertising, it was hard, at first, for Scott to go into this field. But working as a newspaper reporter, technical writer, and college instructor made him appreciate the succinct expression of ideas in magazine ads; he found it a challenge to go from 3500 words to 350. Advertising also gave him the opportunity to use his musical talent, which he had developed by going back to school for a second degree in musical composition (his first was in English).

Of self-employment, Scott says, "I like having customers much more than I liked having bosses." His decision to become a freelancer gained strength after repeated observations that having a job did not guarantee security. Among the joys of his work, Scott lists variety, travel, making his own hours, and working with clients he likes on projects that are either creatively or financially rewarding (and sometimes both).

Among the disadvantages are occasionally crazy hours and the feast-or-famine nature of self-employment, which makes him afraid to turn down work and always cautious about spending. At times he makes little progress on his musical, because he is so exhausted from writing all day that he doesn't have an ounce of energy to do it again at home at night.

Though Scott has successfully balanced conventional and creative achievement, he says, "The trade-offs are impossible to resolve. Many of my friends chose law school or business school and are now doing better financially. Although they often complain about being unfulfilled, it's hard not to ask, did I do the right thing?"

Career Option 7: Get a Grant or Find a Patron

Another way to finance your creative work is to get a grant or find a patron. Foundations, corporations, and government arts councils often fill the role of patrons today. Chapter 5 has more information on getting grants and locating other kinds of public support.

John Kaplan was a successful photojournalist who thought a grant would give him time to pursue a project in greater depth. As a staff photographer on a Pittsburgh newspaper, he had covered the story of a twenty-one-year-old murder suspect's journey through the legal system, and he proposed to extend his work by photographing diverse twenty-one-year-olds around the country. He was awarded the Nikon/NPPA Documentary Sabbatical Grant, a grant given to increase public understanding of social issues.

The grant enabled John to grow as a photographer and writer and gave him the time to take joyous Walter-Mitty-like learning excursions into other people's lives. The downside was that the newspaper would not support his leave of absence—so he quit his regular job! Two years later, his project was awarded the Pulitzer Prize for Feature Photography. Says John, "Winning the Pulitzer was thrilling and it's certainly a good indicator that I'm on the right track. But any contest is totally subjective—different judges produce different winners. It's best to be driven by your own curiosity. My work helps me in a quest for personal growth."

John's interest in photography began when he was just fourteen, when he got to know the photographers at the newspaper where his mother worked. Mentors there helped him develop his eye. College, internships, and on-the-job training further developed his ability to communicate the truth of others' lives through pictures. John currently freelances as a photographer, writer, and consultant. He also teaches and mentors younger photographers, as a payback for the wonderful help given to him earlier in his career.

Knowing that creative people are often so self-focused that their work is magnificent but irrelevant, John recommends striking a balance between the creative and the practical. It helped him to learn that his readers' needs were the most important. Regarding grantsmanship, John says, "Do your homework. Know the market. Keep your proposal simple, yet with content. But don't presuppose what you think the judging committee is looking for. Original, fresh ideas win grants."

Career Option 8: Create an Unconventional Career

Laurel Gray is an ethnochoreologist. She studies, performs, and choreographs ethnic dances, specializing in women's dances of Central Asia. Often told that she has "too many talents," it has been her life's work to develop and weave together her gifts as a dancer, costumer, teacher, musician, historical researcher, writer, and choreographer. Laurel's work brings together her sensitivity to both sound and sight: "I see colors and lines when I listen to music, when I create a dance."

In 1992, Laurel was invited to spend two years at Tashkent's leading theater studying traditional Uzbek dance. While there she studied dance, lived through cultural transformation in the former Soviet Republic of Uzbekistan, and directed her peak creative achievement to date, a concert featuring forty native dancers. She directed the entire performance, including ten pieces she danced herself, designed all the costumes, and choreographed three solos and seven ensemble dances.

Earlier in her career, Laurel supported herself by managing small ethnic retail stores. She enjoyed the autonomy of setting her own schedule and the sales challenge of winning customers over. During this time, she organized the Tanavar Dance Ensemble and kindled public interest in their work by writing articles for dance magazines. Now she finds that she no longer needs a conventional job to support her dancing career. By giving a concert or offering a weekend seminar at which she teaches and sells videos and cassettes, she makes more money in a weekend than she could in a month of conventional work.

Laurel said she "moved from defeatist to empowered" when she stopped thinking of herself as unemployed and realized she was self-employed. Trade-offs to her choice include no job security and no domestic life, including no husband, children, house, or fancy car. Benefits include freedom for creative expression and the stimulation and romance that come with living and working in exotic places. A cultural ambassador, Laurel feels connected all over the world. Art has made her world a global village. And she possesses a rare and precious inner fulfillment that comes from following her bliss.

> *"I don't want my tombstone to read,*
> *'She had a great retirement plan.'"*
>
> —LAUREL GRAY

Commenting that "it's not failure that destroys artists, it's success," Laurel's advice for performing artists is to stay focused and develop inner balance. "It's easy to become distracted and drained by jealous rivals who try to make trouble for you," says Laurel. "Don't take jealousy personally." For dancers she adds, "Dance from your heart; dance to please yourself."

If None of These Options Works for You

Although I highlighted just one approach for each story, you probably noticed that almost all of these successful people used several of the approaches—sometimes simultaneously, sometimes sequentially, changing from one route to another as their interests shifted or their careers blossomed. You too can combine strategies. Many Artistic types actually **prefer** arrangements of different kinds of work in their careers, because different kinds of work provide ways to express different parts of themselves that a single conventional career would stifle.

Let me provide an example of someone I know whose career reflects just this sort of combined arrangement. Andrea Taylor is a fine artist in Pittsburgh to whom I take prints that I'd like framed. She supports herself in many of the ways described above. She sells some of her paintings and does others on commission. She teaches art appreciation for an extended studies program. She combines self-employment and bread-and-butter work as a custom framer in her own shop. And she dabbles in music, currently playing the recorder as a hobby.

If you like the idea of having a creative hobby, but you aren't sure where to begin, look through the occupations listed in chapter 3, keeping your special sensitivities in mind. Maybe you'd enjoy auctioneering. Or puppeteering. Maybe it would be fun to dress as a gypsy and go to local fairs and read palms or crystal balls, or to work as a volunteer, drawing silhouettes for parents of children who are hospitalized. Or maybe this is a good time to begin that hobby you've been putting off for awhile now.

If none of the bread-and-butter options appealed to you, it may be that **where** you work is more important than **what** you do. Perhaps your survival job should be in a setting that relates to your talent. If you are a visual artist, for example, you might look into work at private art galleries, where you can crate and uncrate paintings, make professional contacts, and learn what happens behind-the-scenes. Or you could work in an art museum as a tour guide, custodian, guard, or janitor. Or you could assist a well-known artist in his or her studio. Or you could open your own gallery.

If bread-and-butter work is a necessity for you, but you are not sure of your secondary Holland theme, you could order the Self-Directed Search (800-331-TEST). And/or you could do the skills analysis in

Parachute and *How to Create a Picture*, to become more aware of your other talents.

If you have several ideas in mind, but you're not sure which to pursue, try them all. In *Earning Money Without a Job*,[26] Jay Conrad Levinson suggests lots of options for people who'd like to work for themselves. It's a good book to consult if you'd like ideas for freelancing or single-person businesses. He also recommends that you list many ways you could earn money and then simultaneously do **all five** of your favorite ways. As he points out, income from many jobs increases your security and decreases your dependence on any one job. Besides, some of the five may not work out.

If you are Enterprising as well as Artistic, it may be that your niche lies in bringing together creative talent and commercial opportunity. For example, Jim Rouse is an American entrepreneur who has brought artists and entertainers into shopping areas, boosting sales through public festivals, participatory theater, and crafts workshops. Michael Ovitz, when he was head of Creative Artists Agency, made plans to program movies and TV shows and interactive games for the information highway as a way to provide work for his creative clients.

Another option is to redesign your current job. You may be able to get more of what you want in your present job if you negotiate with your employer. For example, you might change your role at work, or find ways to increase variety or independence on the job. Or maybe you could change your hours or place of work. Job-sharing has become increasingly popular (and was the proposition agreed to by my employer when I needed time to write this book). If it is mutually beneficial, job redesign can save you the stress of a major transition.

It may be that you are not happy with any of the options presented because you don't like the trade-offs involved. People with the most exciting and glamorous careers usually make sacrifices in their personal lives. People who do intrinsically satisfying creative work often make less money than their more extrinsically motivated conventional counterparts. You may not be able to have everything you want, but you can set priorities and devote your time and energy to getting what you want the most. The next chapter will help you learn how.

PART THREE

Making It Happen

"Even if you're on the right track, you'll get run over if you just sit there!"

—WILL ROGERS

You Can Get There from Here!

ONCE YOU HAVE UNDERSTOOD HOW TO MATCH the unique person you are to the world of work, and you have chosen the kind of work or combination of work you want to do, it's time to take action. No one will *offer* you the unique career niche you can create for yourself, but you can learn how to make it happen on your own. This chapter contains specific suggestions for how you can set off, stay on track, and keep moving forward.

A couple of years ago I attended a seminar on creative careers. The speakers were successful professionals from a variety of Artistic occupations—print and broadcast media, public relations, advertising—who had gathered to tell a group of college students how to get into creative fields. They gave tips on the importance of collecting clips to build a portfolio and volunteering or interning as a way to get experience and meet others. By far the most commonly repeated bit of advice from these successful people to the students was to **keep at it...don't give up.** "If you want to do creative work like mine," they said, "you've got to persevere."

Unfortunately, persistence is much easier to talk about than it is to accomplish. One cloth designer was so discouraged after three years of trying to sell her exotic silk-screened fabric that she very nearly gave up. But she kept at it—and her fourth year of business was so successful that now she can't keep up with demand. Like this designer, you may find your persistence to be just as important as your talent if you want to be successful in unconventional ways.

The career goal itself looks terrific, but it's in the distance. The road to your goals will undoubtedly be beset with flat tires, detours, wrong turns, and miles of tedium. You move along smoothly for awhile, and then life happens: Your marriage breaks up. Your car gets totalled. Your child gets sick. Your relatives need care. Financial hardship intensifies other stresses. Even if there are no outstanding problems, a tidal wave of maintenance work almost drowns you, and productivity becomes a luxury.

> *"Nothing in the world can take the place of persistence.*
> *Talent will not; nothing is more common than unsuccessful*
> *men with talent. Genius will not; unrewarded genius is almost*
> *a proverb. Education will not; the world is full of*
> *educated derelicts. Persistence and determination are omnipotent.*
> *The slogan 'press on' has solved and always will solve*
> *the problems of the human race."*
>
> —ATTRIBUTED TO CALVIN COOLIDGE

There is no way to prevent these big and little stresses that distract or derail us from our long-range goals. What we need is a way to persist in pursuit of our favorite possibilities. Let's pull out a very practical map designed by therapists and self-help groups like Weight Watchers and Alcoholics Anonymous—people who know what works when it comes to making positive life changes. Because this map has been drawn by so many sources, it looks like a bit of a hodge-podge. It is organized in two broad categories of positive coping: thinking constructively and finding help. I recommend that you practice both strategies.

> *"If a man advances confidently in the direction of his dreams,*
> *and endeavors to live the life which he has imagined, he will*
> *meet with a success unexpected in common hours."*
>
> —HENRY DAVID THOREAU

Think Constructively

Set goals

Often in counseling, when clients tell me that they don't know what they want, I find that they *do* know what they want—they just don't want to admit it. They think, for reasons that fade under close scrutiny, that they shouldn't want what they want or that they won't be able to get what they want. They are prejudiced against themselves. I remember one client reluctantly admitting—as though it were completely unacceptable—that she wanted to live in the country and have a big vegetable garden and be a good nurse and mother! It surprised her to learn that what she wanted sounded perfectly reasonable to me.

Sometimes people reject their goals because they believe that having a goal means they are committed to it forever. But it's okay to change your goals once you've begun. It's okay to go back and reevaluate. Setting goals and priorities is more of a process than a final decision. You may think you want one thing, but then change your mind once life experience shows you otherwise. Better to have goals and change them than to have no goals at all.

Goals are helpful because they set direction, limits, constraints. Goals are like the banks of a river, without which the river would lose its momentum and direction. Although limits have a negative connotation, they can be very helpful. In *The Courage to Create,* Rollo May illustrates the energy-depleting effects of the "you-can-do-anything" approach: "It's like putting someone into a canoe and pushing him out into the Atlantic toward England with the cheery comment, 'The sky's the limit.'"[27]

When I talk to creative people who have been successful in their careers, they tell me of moments when they said to themselves, "I want to learn to think like an artist," or "I have to master these dances," or "I want to learn to play folk music." They didn't feel pushed by outside forces or compelled to follow a course of action because they "should." They felt a motivation that pulled them from within. They knew what they wanted and their goals followed naturally.

After reading the last chapter, you may already have made some tentative career choices. Once you know your career goals, **write them down.** You can continue to revise and reword them over time, and you may even change them completely. For now, though, do they give you both a sense of direction and more than one way to succeed? As Jerald Forster points out, goals need to be both directional and flexible. An example of a goal that is directional but not flexible is "I want to work for the Royal Shakespeare Company." (What if they don't hire you?) An example of a goal that is flexible but provides no direction is "I want to be rich and famous." (Now what do you do?)

102

You want your goal to give you both a sense of what to do next and the ability to get what you want in more than one way. For example, when I realized that I didn't want to teach English anymore, I expressed my goals this way: "I want to go into counseling and learn more about psychology." From there I was able to make my goals more clear and specific: "I need to go back to graduate school, and I have different programs in different schools from which to choose." (Only then did I learn that there was a field called counseling psychology!) Try to make your goals clear and specific enough that you will know when you have achieved them.

Not everyone sets goals in a straightforward fashion. The following exercise is designed for those of you who prefer a more intuitive and holistic approach. This exercise is something I adapted from other exercises involving focusing, guided imagery, and values clarification.[28] This exercise has been quite popular when I've used it with members of my career groups. Some participants go deeply into the experience and find it very valuable, although on the other hand, it doesn't work at all for an occasional few.

To do this exercise, you and another person with whom you feel comfortable need to set aside some time. Decide ahead of time whether you want to visualize one, two, or three goals, and allow about twenty minutes for each. If you are not sure, plan to do two, one for a personal goal and one for a professional goal. Ask your helper to read from the script below. After you've gone through the entire exercise for the first goal, repeat it for the second goal, and so on. Your helper will need a watch with a second hand. (If you prefer, you could make an audiotape of yourself reading from the script, and then play it back, so that you can be your own guide). Before you begin, dim the lights, unplug the phone, and find a comfortable position. You might lie on a couch, sit in a comfortable chair, or sprawl on the floor. Have a paper and pencil ready.

GUIDED IMAGERY/FOCUSING EXERCISE

Find a comfortable position. Begin to shift your awareness from being outside, in the world, to inside yourself. You may want to close your eyes. Take a couple of deep, slow breaths. Notice if there is any tension in your body. Check your arms and legs, shoulders, and face. Let go of any tension you feel. Breathe out tension; breathe in relaxation.

(pause for 10 seconds)

Feel the tension flowing out; feel the relaxation flowing in. Let yourself relax. It may help to tell yourself something like, "I feel quiet and peaceful and relaxed."

(pause for 20 seconds)

Imagine that you have come into possession of a unique map, designed just for you. It could look like an old pirate map with a buried treasure; it could look like an architect's blueprint; it could be a computer screen with colored graphics; it could be pencil scribbles on a scrap of notebook paper. Take a moment to imagine what your map looks like.

(pause for 15 seconds)

You begin to follow your map and you notice that you are going through some of your favorite territory. You could be walking along the beach, wandering through the forest, floating on a cloud, or venturing into cyberspace. As you go, feelings and thoughts come to you in different ways. They may appear as physical sensations in the body, as words, colors, music, sounds, or images. Let yourself notice what comes to you.

(pause for 10 seconds)

You may notice that you are feeling heavy, perhaps because you are carrying worries or tensions from the day. Look down at your hands and see if you have some baggage you don't really need. If so, load your worries and tensions into your bag and leave them right there. They will be waiting for you when you return.

(pause for 10 seconds)

After leaving your worries behind, you may notice that your step is lighter, that you are now breathing more easily and deeply, that your mind is focused on the future. Continue following your map. You are going deeper and deeper into your favorite territory, where you feel more and more in touch with yourself.

104

(pause for 15 seconds)

Gradually you realize that the map is leading you to your dreams. Pause for a moment and let yourself dream. What do you really want in your life? Consider your sensitivities, the problems that most motivate you, the kind of person you want to be and the things you want to do.

What are your two (or three) most important dreams? Mull them over. There is no need to rush. When you do settle on your choices, write each one down. Start each dream-goal with the words "I want" and write it in clear, specific language in the present tense.

(pause for 5 minutes)

You have written two or three life goals that are very important to you. Now you are going to imagine that the first one comes true.

But first, *make sure that you are in a comfortable position. Take a couple deep breaths. Breathe out tension; breathe in relaxation. It may help to tell yourself that you are feeling very relaxed.

(pause for 20 seconds)

Close your eyes again and imagine that your first (second, third) dream has come true.

(pause for 30 seconds)

Where are you? *(10 seconds)*
What are you doing? *(10 seconds)*
Who, if anyone, is with you? *(10 seconds)*

---

* When you repeat this exercise for further dreams, you will return to this point.

As you imagine your dreams come true, tune into your thoughts and feelings, words, colors, sounds, and images. It would be too hard to divide your goal into parts and imagine each part separately. But you don't have to do that. Imagine the whole of it, and let yourself experience your dream as though it were real.

(pause for 1 minute)

As you imagine your dream, you may find that one particular emotion or sensation appears. Allow yourself to become more aware of that one particular emotion or sensation.

105

(pause for 1 minute)

Attend to one emotion or one sensation and the words or pictures that go with it. Let it change or transform itself into something new, if it wants to do that.

(pause for 1 minute)

See if there is an image that expresses what you are experiencing right now. Let a symbol come to you which expresses your feelings about this life goal.

(pause for 1 minute)

Take a moment to write or draw anything you'd like to. Then we will go on to your next dream. (Allow some time and then begin reading at the ★ and repeat the exercise.)

Don't spend much time thinking about these instructions before you do this exercise. You can do this exercise now and again at other times. If you do the exercise as it is written, you will probably come away with at least one personally meaningful symbol. Sometimes people think that they did not get a symbol at the end, but what often happens is that the symbol comes very quickly and they reject it at first.

Deliberately recall this symbol (it may sound cornball, but it helps!) to remind you of your personal/career goals. One of my clients visualized a tree, rooted and strong, lifting its branches to the sun. She often used this symbol to center herself and stay true to her career goals when family conflict weakened her confidence and resolve. I have done a couple exercises like this in the past ten years and find that all my memorable symbolic images, both personal and professional, either have already come true or are now coming true!

If you are stuck (i.e, you still don't know what you want) and you'd like more help with setting goals, I can recommend a couple of excellent resources. Barbara Sher has written two practical and inspirational self-help manuals for turning dreams into realities: *Wishcraft: How to Get What You Really Want* [29] and *I Could Do Anything If I Only Knew What it Was.*[30]

If you'd like something shorter, I recommend the goal-setting exercises created by Jerald Forster, my professor at the University of Washington. His "Goals Review and Organizing Workbook" (GROW) is designed to help you identify your natural goals. The "Self-Articulation Process" can help you develop positive self-concepts about both your goals and your strengths. Both exercises can be ordered by writing to Jerald Forster, Ph.D., Department of Educational Psychology, University of Washington, Seattle, WA 98195.

> *"If you have built castles in the air, your work need not be lost;*
> *that is where they should be.*
> *Now put the foundations under them."*
>
> —HENRY DAVID THOREAU

Make a timeline and subdivide

Once you've set your goals, make a timeline. First decide on the end date, the time by which you hope to have accomplished your goal. Now divide your overall goal into smaller chunks. Set times by which you hope to have each part accomplished. You need to know not only what you hope to accomplish, but by when. As you get closer to the tasks to be done, keep dividing into smaller chunks, so that you know what you hope to accomplish on a monthly, weekly, daily, even hourly basis. The tasks need to be so small that you know you could do them today. Redo your timeline when you get off schedule.

Many people find that getting started is the hardest part. By setting doable smaller goals, you make it easier to get started. Once you have accomplished the first step, no matter how short the distance, you'll have greater motivation and energy for the rest of the journey. So learn to set realistic goals that are neither too ambitious nor too easy. With practice, you'll get better at setting the right amount of task for the time.

"You have to act to actualize."

—TEDDY FAKLES

107

Increase your desire for your goal

It's hard to stay focused on your goals in the midst of living everyday life. The pressure to pay the bills, stop the children from squabbling, get the cat to the vet, etc., etc., etc., can be tremendously distracting. You will help yourself persist if you do some deliberate things to keep your goals in mind. For example, you can write them on a card and keep the card in your shirt pocket or in your appointment book. Or hang it on the refrigerator door or your computer screen, or dangle it from the rear view mirror in your car. Put it someplace where you will see it frequently.

You can consciously choose to make progress toward your goals instead of drifting into what comes naturally at the moment. "Tonight," you can tell yourself, "I am going to put my goals first. I am going to spend the next ten minutes (or one hour or entire evening) writing this cover letter. I am not going to go to the mall or watch TV or gossip on the phone with my friend." It's like telling yourself that because you want to lose ten pounds by summer, you are not going to eat that bag of M&Ms right now. You put the distant goals before the immediate moment.

You can also consciously strengthen your reasons for attaining your goals. Why do you want to do creative work? Is it because you want to learn new skills, to grow as a person, to feel more whole, to raise your self-esteem? Or do you want to show your children that it's possible to express themselves in constructive ways? Choose reasons that are true for you and important to you and tell them to yourself when you want to increase your motivation. Make your creative goals MORE important to you by the ways you think about them and the things you tell yourself.

You can also instill hope for yourself through examples of other people who have made their dreams a reality. There are people whose aspirations were similar to your own and who have made their dreams come true; you can read their stories and tell yourself, "If they could do it, I can do it too." The people in chapter 4 are examples of real people like you and me who have successfully put their talents to work. There are many more. When you read stories in newspapers or magazines about people whose creativity you admire, cut the articles out and save them in a scrapbook. Talk to them in person, if possible. Feed your hope with real-life success stories.

My colleague Marti Moore recommends creating a career notebook, in which you keep such items as relevant articles from newspapers and magazines, notes about job-related activities you've enjoyed and/or been told you were good at, drafts of resumes, materials from career workshops, research on various careers, and lists of your long- and short-term goals. You might also include your own drawings or writings and other sources of creative inspiration. Such a notebook can help remind you what you want, and show your progress.

Resist perfectionism

In part, perfectionism is inherent in the nature of the creative task. Reaching for an ideal and bringing your ideas to excellence require perfectionistic tendencies and at the same time engender frustration, because making mistakes is also built into the creative process. But sometimes the hunger for perfection is so powerful that we become passive, because only by doing nothing can we avoid the possibility of making an error. Then, unfortunately, we stop learning and growing.

> *"The books I haven't written are better than the books other people have."*
>
> —CYRIL CONNOLLY

In literature, greatness is not equal to perfection. *Hamlet* and *Huckleberry Finn,* for example, are universally agreed to be great works of fiction—and yet volumes have been written about their flaws and imperfections. If you want to make a great contribution, your work doesn't need to be perfect, and neither do you. It's a good thing, too, because the concept of perfection just doesn't apply to human nature. It's like applying the concept of nobility to a rutabaga.

If perfectionism is a problem for you, consult the chapter entitled "Dare to Be Average," in David Burns' best-selling, straight-thinking book, *Feeling Good.*[31] Let me quote from the last paragraph in that chapter:

> In fact, just think what it would be like if you *were* perfect. There'd be *nothing* to learn, *no way* to improve, and life would be completely void of challenge and the satisfaction that comes from mastering something that takes effort. It would be like going to kindergarten for the rest of your life. You'd know all the answers and win every game. Every project would be a guaranteed success because you would do everything correctly. People's conversations would offer you nothing because you'd already know it all. And most important, nobody could love or relate to you. It would be impossible to feel any love for someone who was flawless and knew it all.

Learn to validate yourself

In general, people who take a conventional approach get approval from others as a matter of course. One of the best conventional things I ever did was to have a baby, and I enjoyed all the positive attention and approval I received during pregnancy and early motherhood. On the other hand, people who take an unconventional approach are likely to meet with disapproval or total disinterest. When I was beginning to think about writing this book, for example, most people responded to my enthusiasm with polite disinterest. If I had needed people to respond to my writing goals the way they responded to the baby, I never would have written this book.

If your creative work has not yet brought you approval, try patting your own back. Tell yourself what a good idea it is and how well you are doing. Remind yourself that you're a swan, not an ugly duckling. When people ask you what you do, say "I'm a cartoonist," or "I'm working on creative solutions to the problem of overpopulation." Define yourself by something you feel good about. Don't define yourself exclusively by your day job title, especially if it's one that makes you feel apologetic.

Think about what success means to you. Once you have independently defined it, it will bother you less if you are not successful by conventional standards. Many people feel like failures because they are measuring themselves against an obsolete model of career advancement. How many people do you know whose career progress looks like the trail of a rocket? Today's career path looks more like a spider web, says life/work planner and trainer Fontelle Gilbert.

Once you are past basic security needs, happiness seems to be more about doing than having, anyway. What I do with my time thirty-five or more hours a week feels more important to me than what kind of a car I drive. When I asked some conventionally successful people what they wanted for their children, they did not say, "I want them to have a six-figure salary and an estate like mine." On the contrary, they said they wanted their children to work at something important to them to which they had to give their all.

As philosopher Mickey Perloff puts it, "Nobody gets a guarantee they made the right choices." You have chosen a difficult, nonlinear path, and you can expect times when you feel down and times when the work is not going well. Anticipating difficulties makes them easier to bear. You'll have difficulties because that's life and that's the nature of the creative process, not because there is something wrong with you.

"Sad to say, the road to good intentions is paved with hell."

—LEE ROY BEACH

You might even consider *planning* for difficulties and setbacks. Alan Marlatt and Judith Gordon are psychologists who have pioneered the study of relapse prevention.[32] They make a distinction between lapses and relapses. When people try to change their habits, they often fail. That's human and to be expected: We all make mistakes. However, people get in trouble when they interpret a single mistake as a total failure, then abandon all further effort, instead of turning the mistake into an opportunity for learning.

For example, suppose that to pursue your creative goals you want to talk to an important person in your field. But you don't, because you feel too shy. To keep the lapse (not calling one time) from becoming a total failure (never calling at all), have a strategy worked out, so you know how you will respond when your actions don't reflect your good intentions. Maybe, for example, you could start by contacting someone less intimidating, or writing down what you want to say and practicing with a friend. Commit yourself to getting back on track as soon as possible after a lapse, and then congratulate yourself for having done it. It may help you to know that when it comes to changing habits, the more you try, the better your chances for success.

111

Find Help

Everyone—even self-sufficient creative types—can benefit from the help provided by other people. The stresses of life are easier to bear when you have supportive people to share your joys and sorrows and offer practical assistance. Most people get social approval just from behaving conventionally. Any college student knows that having a safe, recognizable major that is presumed to lead to gainful employment will elicit approving comments from parents and friends. If you choose an unconventional path, though, you may need to be quite deliberate about garnering support. Suggestions follow on the kinds of support that are most likely to be helpful to you.

If the idea of finding help sounds like using people, remember that any good and lasting relationship is mutually beneficial: You will get support but you will also give it. Although I tend to be idealistic about relationships, at their core I see some version of "You scratch my back and I'll scratch yours." Sounds unromantic, but relationships work best when they meet mutual needs.

Sometimes creative and unconventional people fail to nurture the supportive relationships that are available to them. They deny their need for help and bend over backward to be independent, and their interpersonal needs go underground in fantasies of fame and fortune. But, as psychologist Ann Kimber so astutely notes, acclaim from afar is not the same as helpful relationships in real life. Worse yet, acclaim based on achievement is conditional. As a star college quarterback once commented, he was only as popular as his last pass. Furthermore, celebrity status offers no buffer to the stresses of everyday life. As a glance at any tabloid will tell you, the rich and famous are as vulnerable as the rest of us to divorce, depression, drug abuse, and disease.

At the Academy Awards, the winners thank their mentors, family, and friends. They are the first to say they didn't do it alone. You don't have to do it alone, either. You can ask for help.

Find someone who believes in your ability to create

Every artist—and that includes you—benefits from at least one supportive person who believes in their ability to create. That person could be your parent, your spouse, your therapist, your friend…it really doesn't matter, as long as they are there for you and believe in you. You can get along without it if you have to, but the stresses of the creative role will be harder to bear. You can't make this kind of relationship happen, but you can nurture it when it comes along.

Learn to work with a critic

It's surprisingly hard to get candid objective criticism. Many people can't be critical, either because they are afraid of damaging the relationship or because they just don't think critically. Objective, external feedback can help you refine and improve your creative work. A true critic can help you in ways that you can't help yourself, while preserving your self-esteem and even enhancing your relationship. Find someone who is willing and able to give you the kind of feedback you need, and then nurture and develop the relationship.

One of my hobbies is decorating my own home. I have a vision of how I want things to look, and I enjoy selecting and arranging colors and patterns and textures and so on. To help me achieve my goals, I have developed a relationship with an interior designer who functions as a critic. She has more experience and more knowledge than I do, and she

can provide feedback on my ideas and suggest alternatives when necessary. I trust her to help me make esthetic choices, which I greatly appreciate when I'm spending real money.

Develop a relationship with a mentor

Mentors are people whose work you admire, individuals who are farther
along a career path similar to your own and thus able to offer both wis-
dom and practical guidance. Their vision and encouragement can enlarge
your sense of the possibilities. Mentors are often real people that you
know—such as teachers or experts or innovators in your field.

113

If you haven't yet got a relationship with a real-life mentor, you could
use your imagination to develop a relationship with a symbolic mentor.
One experimental psychologist claimed as her mentor a renowned
woman psychologist she did not know personally but whose research she
admired. One of my clients, a writer and diarist, told me that she found
a kind of mentor in that great character of children's fiction, Harriet the
Spy. When others found and read her diary, she remembered how Harriet
had survived a similar misfortune.

Join a support group

"Isolation is the dream killer," says team-builder Barbara Sher. If you feel
alone in your struggle to create an unconventional niche for yourself, find
a group of people in the same boat. Look for people who are like you,
who share your values, who can offer emotional support and receive your
support as well. A group of like-minded people can provide the approval
and assistance you don't receive from the conventional world. These days
more and more people are finding support through online Internet discussion groups. A formal support group is another possibility, but so are
associations and an informal network of peers, people that you bring
together by calling them and arranging to meet for lunch.

Make a contract with others

If you have told others what you hope to accomplish and have made a
contract with them, you'll be more likely to achieve your goals than if
you had simply made a promise to yourself. Weight Watchers uses this

principle when they have dieters weigh in at meetings. Find a person or a group to whom you can report, and set up a regular meeting time. Tell them what you expect to do in the coming week and ask them to check your progress the following week. This is more fun if they too are working towards a goal and they can check in with you.

Take advantage of public support

Some social service agencies exist to support creative endeavors. Contact your state arts council. It will be in the phone book with other state agencies, with a name something like Commission on Arts, Council on the Arts, or Arts Board. Some state arts funds come from the National Endowment for the Arts, which provides financial assistance in the form of fellowships, grants, and studio space. These funds are released to institutions, groups, and individuals. You can register with your state agency to receive information on new opportunities.

Some state arts councils sponsor Artist-in-Residence programs. Public schools, art schools, university art departments, and other organizations offer short-term residencies to artists and other creators. Your state arts council can also give you information on the Art in Public Places program, which is funded by the General Services Administration (GSA). The GSA is permitted to spend a small percentage of federal construction monies on art.

Your librarian can help you locate more information on public support. Ask to see a foundation directory. It lists foundations that support the arts, such as the Guggenheim, Rockefeller, and Ford Foundations.

Write to the National Network for Artist Placement, 935 West Avenue 37, Los Angeles, CA 90065. Or call (213) 222-4035. From NNAP you can order internship directories and resource guides and career handbooks devoted specifically to film, theater, dance, or fine arts. They have information on resources and job opportunities in acting, arts administration, dance, design, folk arts and crafts, general arts, literary arts, media arts, music, performing arts, photography, theater arts, and visual arts.

The Actors' Fund provides a range of social services to entertainers who are ill or unemployed. Their headquarters is at 1501 Broadway, Suite 518, New York, NY 10036; their phone number is (212) 221-7300.

If These Suggestions Don't Work for You

Even if it seems like none of these strategies will work for you, adopt a trial-and-error approach. Try them all. Some will work better than others. Adapt those that work somewhat so they work even better, and then spend more of your time on the strategies that work best for you. Remember, too, that your behavior does not depend on your emotional state. You can feel unhappy, miserable, negative, and scared and still take steps that will move you closer to your goals. In fact, taking action can have a positive effect on your feelings.

In situations that make you feel anxious, try taking small, well-planned steps to get around the obstacles or fears blocking your path. As you gain experience and confidence, you'll be able to take larger steps and bolder risks. For example, a poet might start writing only for him- or herself, then progress to sharing a single poem with a trusted friend, then asking for feedback on a work in progress from a small writer's group, and so on, before finally performing in public. (One woman I know of took this a step further—after following all these steps, she then booked her first reading without telling her friends or family. That way, she figured, if she was a failure, no one she cared about would know. When the evening went well, she felt comfortable inviting everyone she knew to her second reading.)

> *"Fear stops action. Action cures fear."*
>
> —MARGARET BOURKE-WHITE

> *"Whatever you think you can do or believe you can do,*
> *begin it. Action has magic, grace, and power in it."*
>
> —JOHANN GOETHE

If you have tried different ways to think constructively and find help but you are stuck and can't seem to get going, you probably need to focus less on what you are doing and attend more to the context in which you are acting. It's like the shift from figure to ground in those optical illusions where if you look one way, it's the profile of two women, and if you look the other way, it's a vase. So let's shift now to the ground on which you take action.

Get professional help

Therapists are professionals who can help you in many different ways. They may see what you can't see. If you think you are doing everything right but something's clearly wrong, it may be that, like most of us, you have psychological problems of which you are not aware. Self-help books can help you with the conscious tasks of advancing your career, but they probably can't help you become aware of the unconscious ways you contribute to your problems. And if you are not aware, there is nothing you can do.

I've worked with many people who were clinically depressed who didn't think they were depressed because they did not feel sad. But they did feel empty or numb, and very tired. Although pep talks and appeals to their willpower couldn't snap them out of it, a therapeutic relationship and sometimes an antidepressant helped them get back on track. If you are not moving forward with your career because you are too tired to move *anywhere,* you may need treatment for depression as a first step.

Many therapists are relationship experts. If you have trouble maintaining relationships that nurture and support you, therapy can help you with that. A therapist can teach good interpersonal skills through modeling, role-playing, reinforcement, and feedback on how you come across. If you currently lack the support you need, a therapist can substitute for your support network and fill the roles of mentor, external monitor, and person who believes in your ability to create. They can also help you locate support groups and other community resources.

The best way to find a therapist is by personal referral. Kooks and flakes seem to be overrepresented in the ranks of therapists, and as a buyer you need to beware. If you don't trust your therapist, talk to them about it, and if the problem doesn't clear up, leave. Whether your therapist is a career counselor, clinical social worker, licensed psychologist, or even a psychiatrist, the letters behind their name are less important than the quality of relationship you have with them. There are competent and not so competent helpers in all fields.

Don't abuse drugs and alcohol

History is filled with romantic, rebellious images of artists as drunks and drug-users and, indeed, creative and unconventional people often seem to be drawn to substance abuse. Perhaps it has to do with this mystique, or with the notion that rules and guidelines are for other, more conventional people. Just be aware, however, that no matter how much of a free spirit you are, you aren't likely to move forward in life if your brain is awash in alcohol or other drugs. People who use substances tend to move backwards, rather than forwards, as their substance abuse creates new problems to compound the ones they are avoiding through intoxication. Drug and alcohol abuse creates problems such as loss of jobs or relationships, all kinds of accidents, and a greater likelihood of crime and family violence. You know you are dependent when you need more drugs or alcohol to get the same effects and if you experience withdrawal when you no longer use them.

117

Even if you have the I.Q. of a genius, you can't expect your brain to function up to its potential if it's swimming in a sea of toxic substances. If you have been abusing substances, try the suggestions in this chapter *after* you stop. You'll get better results. If you find that you aren't able to maintain reasonable limits, seek professional help or join a self-help group such as Alcoholics Anonymous.

Get into a safe environment

It's difficult to pursue your dreams if you live in fear that you are going to be beaten or raped or killed. Just as plants need water and sunshine, human beings need safety to grow and learn. It's not your fault if you are not safe, but it is your responsibility to move yourself into a new environment where you *will* be safe. Getting safe may mean leaving people and places you love and losing your familiar world, but it has to be done if you want to live your creative dreams. Without safety, the suggestions in this chapter won't help much.

Develop your character

If you've tried the strategies suggested here and find that you are not getting what you want, it may be that these tips and tactics don't go deep
enough. You may need to attend to that bedrock from which your
actions spring—your character. Character is hard to define, but for me it
has to do with integrity, with doing what you say you will do, and with
being honest in your presentation of yourself. Integrity emanates from
people with character, making it easy to trust them. And trust is vital to
relationships. Without trust, your relationships won't be mutually beneficial, and your progress depends on good relationships.

> *"Style is character. A good style cannot come from a bad,*
> *undisciplined character."*
>
> —NORMAN MAILER

As Stephen Covey points out in *The Seven Habits of Highly Effective
People,*[33] the success literature of the past fifty years oversells tricks and
gimmicks at the expense of character development. If you want to develop your character, *Seven Habits* provides principles that when diligently
followed become habits leading to personal integrity. These principles are
arranged in sequence, bringing inner security before external achievement. Like *Parachute* and other great career books, *Seven Habits* advocates
discovering and honoring your personal mission in life and treating other
people with decency and consideration.

Give yourself time

If your destination is clear and you are taking the necessary steps, but you
don't feel like you are getting closer to your goals, you may not have
given yourself enough time. After all, this whole chapter has been about
delayed gratification. If your aspirations are to greatness, you will need to
give yourself many years before you see big results. Benjamin Bloom
found that people who had achieved world-class status in their respective
fields had spent at least ten years during which they had "devoted more
time, energy, and thought to their talent areas than to any other activity
or area of their lives."[34]

Since gratification in the form of public acclaim may be a long time in coming, it's important to find ways to gratify yourself all along. A life of rigorous discipline and unending hardship can be unnecessarily bleak and even counterproductive. Find little ways to reward yourself every day. You might schedule something you enjoy—such as meeting a friend or taking a walk—after a block of time devoted to your career goals. And when something goes really well for you, celebrate! Invite your helpers and supporters to celebrate with you.

You may feel at this point that creating an unconventional niche for yourself is just way more work than you bargained for. I can't blame you. I can't tell you the number of times I've wished it was easier myself. But I don't believe quick and easy success is possible. The people whose success I respect made real and often unglamorous contributions day in and day out. Their success was not the miraculous result of a flash-in-the-pan dynamic personality or beliefs in inspirational messages. I don't believe your success will be either.

Henry Geldzahler observed the career development of visual artists over many years. Previously curator at the Metropolitan and Director of Visual Arts for the National Endowment for the Arts, Geldzahler was commissioner of cultural affairs of the City of New York when he wrote:

> ...it is not the cunning careerist who wins in the end. It is the careful nurturer who tills his garden daily and grows the most natural, organic, and unforced flowers—the most beautiful ones and those most aesthetically 'necessary' and satisfying. A successful career is, most often, the result of countless decisions made along the way, decisions that always intuitively support the art and, without ignoring life style, give it the weight it deserves."[35]

"The successful person has the habit of doing the things failures don't like to do," wrote essayist E. M. Gray. "They don't like doing them either necessarily." But they do them. Paradoxically, this hard work isn't as disagreeable as it may sound. Work that is well chosen and at the right level for your abilities can actually be more joyous than getting stoned or watching TV or doing nothing at all. Creative work can nurture your soul in ways our popular diversions never can.

"Man matures through work which inspires him to difficult good."

—POPE JOHN PAUL II

~~~~~~~~~~~~~~

"We make a living by what we get, but we make a life by what we give."

—WINSTON CHURCHILL

Have an Adventure

BY NOW YOU HAVE PROBABLY FIGURED OUT a way to make your unconventionality an advantage in our changing work world. Maybe you know how you want to support yourself and your best strategies for making your dreams come true. But if you are like me you may find that instead of taking action you are gazing at your navel, slightly paralyzed by the uncertainties ahead. This chapter is not so much about taking observable action as it is about finding the inspiration and courage within. Before you're ready to act, you need to take heart.

You may remember Laurel Gray from chapter 4, who was introduced as an example of someone who created her own career. When I interviewed Laurel about her career development, she told me that it helped to think of achieving her career goal as an adventure in Joseph Campbell's mythic sense. She was on a heroic journey—meeting challenges, suffering through adversity, growing as a person.

The journey has long been a popular metaphor for living and learning, helping us to focus on the process and recognize that sometimes there is greater joy in taking the journey than in reaching the destination. Many people have found the reward not so much in the end product as in the person they become and the adventure they enjoy along the way.

Centuries ago, the journey was more than a metaphor for a craftsman. After completing an apprenticeship with a master, the young silversmith or blacksmith or other tradesman literally set out on a journey from town to town, doing whatever work the local townspeople required. During this period, which might last years, the craftsmen refined their skills and gradually mastered their trade. This the original meaning of the word "journeyman," describing someone who is more skilled than a beginner but has not yet reached the level of a master.

Laurel compared her journey to Dorothy's in *The Wizard of Oz*. Before Dorothy and Toto got back to Kansas, and before Laurel got back to the States from Tashkent, they each had an adventure that was both scary and fun. Thinking about your career as an adventure that takes time may help you develop patience with the process.

What lies before you? Let me offer a final map, one that will give you some idea of what to expect on the road to your own personal Oz. More than any of the others, this map is one that you fill in on your own, draw as you go. It is a map that stretches forward in time, charting your lifelong process of changing and growing through creative work. It depicts a developmental process, a work-related unfolding of the self that has many parallels to the creative process. While the process can't be controlled, it can be trusted.

How is your career adventure likely to unfold? Well, like a story, it will have a beginning, a middle, and an end; unlike a story, the end is kind of a non-ending that spirals back to a new beginning. I like the overview provided by author Lewis Hyde. In his book *The Gift,* Hyde identifies three kinds of gifts in a natural progression:

> The initial gift is what is bestowed upon the self—by perception, experience, intuition, imagination, a dream, a vision, or by another work of art.... But it is rare for the initial material to be a finished work of art; we must usually labor with it.
>
> The ability to do the labor is the second gift. The artist works...from that part of our being which is a gift and not an acquisition. To speak of our talents as gifts distinguishes them from those abilities that we acquire through the will.
>
> ...if the artist is gifted, the gift increases in its passage through the self. The artist makes something higher than what he has been given, and this, the finished work, is the third gift, the one offered to the world...[36]

Your creative development may follow a similar process. Let's take a more in-depth look at each stage of the journey.

The Beginning

At the beginning of a creative career, just as at the beginning of a creative project, you may not be able to say exactly what you are doing or how you are going to proceed. The problem itself is not clear. Clients of mine who struggle with this ambiguity tell me they wish their goals were clearer and that they could move more quickly along a straighter path. They wish they felt more secure. They feel distressed, as if something must be "wrong," yet from my perspective their feelings are appropriate and understandable.

123

> *"Works of art are indeed always products of having*
> *been in danger, of having gone to the very end in an experience,*
> *to where man can go no further."*
>
> —RAINER MARIA RILKE

Submitting yourself to the creative process is like falling in love. You feel shaky and uncertain on the inside, especially at the beginning. Joy and transformation await, but first you must take a risk, make yourself vulnerable, and that's scary. There is a natural desire to stay safe and secure, and not to face the unknown. But if you play it safe, you miss out on a great romance.

The artist in your soul may awaken when you encounter the work of a master. You resonate to it, although you may not recognize its importance at the time. I was once part of an audience who had gathered to question a panel of Northwest comedians about how they became successful in their careers. As the comedians answered questions and listened to each other, it dawned on them that they all began their careers as children, when they were inspired by listening to their favorite comedians on the radio. As kids, they did not realize they would eventually become comedians. But later they pointed to those moments as the beginning of their identity.

Your gifts may also be awakened by certain situations that seem mysterious or obviously wrong to you. We usually speak of people finding a problem, but one of my sculptor clients said that the problems always seemed to find her. Maybe you are motivated by an important social need or excited by a revolutionary new idea. Many feminists from many different disciplines became engaged in creative action because of problems related to gender. Roseanne Barr, for example, has said that her drive to do standup comedy grew out of her frustration with the way she was treated as a housewife and mother.

The most important action you can take at the beginning of your journey is to accept your gifts and the difficulties they bring with them. Sometimes gifted people deny their talent because they fear that doing creative work will prevent them from getting something else they want, such as financial security, or the respect of others. But while denial and avoidance may work in the short run, they simply won't work in the long run. Something of the irresistibility of your gifts is implied by the words *vocation* and *occupation*. *Vocation* is defined as a calling; *occupation* means to take possession of, to seize.

If we believe data from the Johnson O'Connor Research Foundation, an organization that has been testing human aptitudes since 1922, it appears that **you can't ignore your talents because they won't ignore you.** Johnson O'Connor researchers have found that people who have ignored their gifts in their career/life planning are frustrated and unhappy by midlife, and they urge that you use your talents either in your job or your hobbies. As the ancient Greek playwrights implied, you can't avoid your fate. In fact, it makes more sense to try loving your fate. Embrace your gifts and the career challenges they present to you.

Theologian Matthew Fox shares the experience of one of his students who had both affirmed and rejected her creative gifts:

> "When I have been attentive to the creative gifts within, I have been free to play and grow as a human being. When I have cooperated in the denial of those gifts, or when I have chosen to set them aside I have withered. My love of life has suffered. I have stopped praying, I have become small and cynical or I have driven myself to the point of exhaustion and burnout. I have become a compulsive worker trying to make up in my work what I have denied in my most creative self." [37]

A career adventure will almost certainly require sacrifice. You may have to let go of something precious to you, such as a romantic self-image. Or financial security. Or social status. Or popularity. Or pleasing your parents. Or enjoying a creative lifestyle until you work out a way to support yourself. "Sacrifice is integral to the nature of vocation. Forfeiting something valued for the sake of someone or something that has greater value or claim is a prerequisite for gaining genuine vocational satisfaction," says educational specialist Sandra Dolan.

Most of us both do and do not want to set off on an adventure. My creative clients come to counseling because they are mired down in depression or self-criticism or bad habits, but when I ask them why they want to get better, they say that they want to help other people, to share their experience, to give freely of their joy and love and talent. That goal gives them incentive to embark on an adventure of personal learning and growth.

The Middle

After accepting the gifts you have been given, you work with them, strengthening them through training and development. You may labor with your gifts through formal education, apprenticeship, independent study and reflection, continuing practice or whatever makes sense to you. You invest your time and energy and other resources to learn your craft and develop your talents.

It doesn't matter whether you labor at work or play (i.e., a hobby). Creative work and play look surprisingly alike, and feel alike as well. Research has shown that people are happiest when they are fully engaged at a task that is intrinsically motivating and set at the frontier of their abilities. This kind of plain hard work actually feels good much of the time. The psychologist Edward Bordin believes that we need to discipline our effort before we can truly enjoy play. A good example would be the musician whose enjoyment in music increases after years of disciplined effort.

If the danger at the beginning of your journey lies in failing to accept your gifts, the danger in the middle is in making them the sole focus of yourself and your life. Creative people are vulnerable to overidentifying with their talent and overinvesting in their work. The sensitivity that makes them special also makes it easier for them to become wounded, to go into a shell. One psychoanalyst wrote:"The tendency to wrap himself in a cloak of narcissistic self-love—because his art in its content is in greater or lesser degree a transformation of himself—in the event of outer rejection is a very powerful one. This is one of the sources of that excessive self-love which destroys art and artists."[38]

> *"Every author, however modest, keeps a most outrageous vanity chained like a madman in the padded cell of his breast."*
>
> —LOGAN PEARSALL SMITH

A very dear friend of mine made this mistake. A person of unusual intellectual and creative gifts, he made being a writer his only identity and achieving recognition for his writing his only real life goal. Perhaps because so much was at stake, he was hypersensitive to the inevitable criticism and rejection his work received. Gradually he withdrew from people and then he even stopped writing. Shortly after turning forty, he killed himself. Certainly many factors influenced his suicide, but I believe one of them was shame that he had not been accorded the recognition of his talent that he'd expected by mid-life.

I tell you his tragic story because it contains a lesson for us all, and I believe he would want you to be helped by it. As a safeguard, my best advice is to spread your eggs out among many different baskets. Some relationship baskets and some just-for-fun baskets; some exciting, creative, this-could-make-you-great baskets and some more ordinary, secure, but still satisfying work baskets. We are all vulnerable to becoming dangerously depressed if we put all our eggs in one basket and then something bad happens to that basket.

> *"I use my talent for writing, but I save my genius for living."*
>
> —OSCAR WILDE

You want to use your creative talents, but not to the exclusion of the rest of yourself. Dick Bolles, the author of *Parachute,* has a nice metaphor for this situation. Suppose that you are a chef, and you have been asked to use a tomato (your creative gift) in tonight's meal. You could use the tomato stuffed as a main course, stewed as a vegetable, tossed in a salad, or simply as a garnish to dress the plate. The important thing is to use it— **along with other foods.** You'd never want it to be the *only* food you served.

The middle of any adventure can be pretty tough going at times, because that's where you spend the most time and encounter the greatest adversity. You will undoubtedly face difficulties on your path: grants that fall through, contracts cancelled, poor ticket sales, not being able to find a job in your field, etc. The preceeding chapter is designed to help you cope with adversity, suggesting lots of ways to persist in spite of difficulties.

If the critics panned your screenplay, it's okay to retreat to a safe place and lick your wounds. Then, when you are ready, you learn what you can from the experience and get back on the road. Learning from experience is one of my favorite definitions of intelligence, and I don't know a more positive way to cope.

The Ending

After accepting and laboring with your gifts, you give something back to the world. There are many ways to give. If you write a poem and have it published, that's sharing a gift. If you are a teacher who instills in your students a love of learning or a librarian who instills in your patrons a love of books and reading, that's sharing a gift. If you design a new piece of farm machinery, something that protects farmers while helping them harvest their crops, that is also sharing a gift.

Giving something back is easier to do once you realize that other people struggle with the same problems you do. Especially when you are young, you feel alone. There was a time, for example, when I felt like I was the only one who didn't fit in. But when you look around, you will see that your personal problem is also a universal problem shared by other

127

people, and you need to generalize your problem so that its solution has relevance for others. That is also the only way your gift can be appreciated; your individual experience takes on meaning for the world when other people can relate.

Albert Camus commented on the necessary tension between the personal and the universal when he accepted the Nobel Prize in 1958:

> "The man who, as often happens, chose the path of art
> because he was aware of his difference soon learns that he
> can nourish his art, and his difference, solely by admitting his
> resemblance to all. The artist fashions himself in that cease-
> less oscillation from himself to others, midway between the
> beauty he cannot do without and the community from
> which he cannot tear himself."

Usually, giving something back to the community feels good. People like your poem or your book selection or your tractor and tell you so. Some creators are exalted, receiving wealth and fame in return for their gifts. We live in the most pluralistic society ever, and I'd be willing to bet that even if your work is not universally admired, you *can* find an audience that will truly appreciate it.

However, giving a gift also carries with it the threat of public censure and disapproval. Our culture *seems* to revere creativity and places it on a pedestal with other socially desirable attributes, such as intelligence, good looks, and extraversion. But society's response to creativity is in fact much more ambivalent. Think about what happened to exceptionally creative people such as Socrates, Jesus Christ, and Galileo. Most of us won't have to worry about being put to death or on house arrest, but we may still occasionally find ourselves very unpopular.

> *"Society is downright savage to creative thinkers,*
> *especially when they are young."*
>
> —PAUL TORRANCE

The danger in the final part of our journey lies in withholding our gifts because we fear we'll be unpopular or disliked or criticized. Society likes conformity, and thus we represent a threat. Creators are typically both an irritant and a catalyst to their world. Most people are disturbed and upset when the status quo is challenged, even if later they appreciate that progress could not otherwise have been made.

> *"The sour truth is that I am imprisoned with a*
> *perception which will settle for nothing less than making a*
> *revolution in the consciousness of our time."*
>
> —NORMAN MAILER

129

I encourage you to offer your gift even if you may face some unfair criticism in return. It's all part of the process, and I don't think other people are intentionally cruel so much as they are human beings who don't like change. I don't always embrace new ideas myself. And when someone conventional has a very negative reaction to one of my ideas and I feel hurt, I tell myself that I must be on target or I wouldn't be getting such an emotional response. In fact, it has often been my experience that someone who is initially very negative later comes around to appreciate the idea very much.

I'd also like to encourage you to approach your own career as an adventure. You are never too old to embark on an adventure. And a journey can be undertaken by everyone, whether they are a neophyte or a superstar.

You can trust and take part in this process. Your gifts will be awakened when you are in the presence of a master. The problems will find you. Your problems will be other people's problems, as well. Your task is to accept your gifts and your problems. Discipline your talent. Generalize your experience. Take risks. Risk investing in the development of your talent, even though you lack any assurance of return. Risk giving something of yourself, even though others may not respond positively.

The End Is a New Beginning

At this point you may be wondering what "career adventure" means for you. You're not sure how much priority you should give to your creative endeavors and how much you should give to a secure job with a decent income. You don't know whether following your bliss means starting a new hobby that fits into your schedule or making a radical change, like going back to school to study architecture.

These kinds of questions reflect the creative process itself. The questions may be more important than the answers, for the answers keep evolving and aren't so much right or wrong as different ways to proceed with different advantages and disadvantages. But the questions beckon you to adventure. So you make the best choices you can at the time and trust the process.

Because you will always be changing and growing as a person, you'll probably find that satisfying your creative urge is not simply a matter of finding an ideal job and living happily ever after. Instead, finding new outlets for your creativity is likely to be an ongoing challenge. It is typical of creative people, even those who are very successful, to want more than is provided in their jobs. Think of the TV stars who abandon roles that may seem to outsiders like the pinnacle of success.

A career adventure focuses on problems to which the answers are never final. Conflicts and contradictions abound, and as you embody those conflicts and grow through them, you realize more of your potential.

Then, from a more mature perspective, you are again faced with the inevitable tensions that are part of being human. There are always new gifts and new problems that emerge and need to be integrated, however much development has already taken place.

Clearly, it's not easy to sustain a creative career adventure. It's a heroic undertaking. There will be times when your adventure is wonderfully fun and exciting, and other times when you need to call on your courage. Psychologist Donald MacKinnon emphasizes the importance of courage for the creator:

> The most salient mark of a creative person, the central trait
> at the core of his being is, as I see it, just this sort of courage.
> It is not physical courage of the type that might be rewarded
> by the Carnegie Medal or the Congressional Medal of
> Honor, although a creative person may have courage of this
> kind, too. Rather, it is personal courage, courage of the mind
> and spirit, psychological or spiritual courage that is the radix
> of a creative person: the courage to question what is general-
> ly accepted; the courage to be destructive in order that
> something better can be constructed; the courage to think
> thoughts unlike anyone else's; the courage to be open to
> experience both from within and from without; the courage
> to imagine the impossible and try to achieve it; the courage
> to stand aside from the collectivity and in conflict with it if
> necessary, the courage to become and to be oneself.[39]

It Takes Courage to Be Yourself

Otto Rank was an early psychologist who wrote about the psychological development of the creative person. According to Rank, there are three kinds of people. He said the **average** person conforms to society to the exclusion of expressing his or her individuality, and the **neurotic** person expresses his or her individuality to the exclusion of being part of society. Only the **artistic** person successfully integrates the two conflicting roles. A later writer summarized Rank's ideas as follows: "The ideal of the average is to be as others are; of the 'neurotic,' to be himself largely in

131

opposition to what others want him to be; of the creative person, to be that which he actually is."[40]

I suppose it would be easier for all of us to be the people we truly are if we didn't inherit so many prejudices about the kind of person we think we *should* be. These internal "shoulds" may be the fiercest lions and tigers and bears you ever encounter. One of my favorite great American novels is *Invisible Man* by Ralph Ellison. The invisible man is an African American and a Southerner who, after trying very hard and unsuccessfully to become the kind of person he thought he should be, concludes, "I yam what I yam."

One of the things I learned as a result of writing this book is to honor creativity in many different forms, both within myself and as a part of everybody I know. A literary snob, I used to think that if I couldn't be Jane Austen or William Shakespeare, I might as well not write. Despite positive feedback from others, I did not take nonfiction writing seriously or appreciate my empathic abilities. Now that I have gone through the process of writing this book, I'm more appreciative that I can make a contribution even if I'm not Jane Austen—and I'm able to look at other people and their gifts with less prejudice as well.

"You need to keep your eye on the ball, not Babe Ruth."

—NANCY PACKER

Perhaps the person you are doesn't fit your image of the person you *want* to be. If so, try to recognize and honor your uniqueness. Nancy McCarthy, a career counselor in the fashion industry, told me that she originally wanted to be an architect, but she didn't have the three-dimensional spatial ability an architect needs. Now she sees herself as having other remarkable gifts and making a greater contribution than she would have made as an architect. John Holland is an Artistic type who gave up aspirations to be a concert pianist because he lacked sufficient musical memory. Instead, he played the piano at home and devoted his genius to the development of a career theory that has helped thousands of people and will doubtless help thousands more.

You too may originally have been inspired by a career choice that was too limiting, perhaps because there were some pieces missing in your understanding of yourself. As you continue your own career adventure, you will come to know yourself well enough to see the highest and most complex use of your gifts, and you can let go of earlier and simpler ideas that prove to be too confining.

> *"I did not make my songs, my songs made me."*
>
> —JOHANN GOETHE

When you call on your courage and set off on your career adventure, you will grow as a person. Like Laurel Gray in chapter 4, you may find that what you thought you were going after is not the greatest thing you achieve. Often, the adversity you encounter on your path may turn out to have unexpected benefits. As Joseph Campbell observed in *The Power of Myth,* "The more challenging or threatening the situation or context to be assimilated and affirmed, the greater the stature of the person who can achieve it. The demon you can swallow gives you its power, and the greater life's pain, the greater life's reply."

It's the challenge of a lifetime: Love your fate. Pursue your unconventional goals. Have an adventure. Realize that you are the artist of your own life. Here's how religious writer Marcus Bach describes the philosophy that life is art:

> I am the artist! I am the master craftsman shaping my existence from the cradle to the grave. I wield the tools, dream the dreams, see the visions, draw the plans, take the time, do the work in everything I say and think every moment of the day. As a sculptor takes his raw material and begins to realize the ideal, or idealize the real, as a painter takes his brush and gives form to his creative idea, so in total life I am the artist![41]

Our World Needs Your Work

Creative work brings things together at many levels. Creative thinking brings information together in a new product. Creative activities bring different parts of yourself together, reclaiming parts that have grown unfamiliar through disuse. A creative approach to life/work planning can bring different kinds of work together in a new career. But creative work also has the power to bring together a world outside ourselves. As we approach the twenty-first century on an overpopulated planet, we surely need the power of creativity to solve our problems, to help us find a unity that honors our diversity.

Ralph Burgard is a policy maker who believes that the arts create social unity. Here are some of his ideas on how to bring art into our culture:

> I recommend that every city immediately hire three additional people: A Curator of Sound, A Curator of Sight, and a Town Fool—unless they already have one.
>
> The Curator of Sound would build ponds to attract the best spring peepers for melodious evenings; would scatter the best bird seed to lure the finest songbirds in all seasons; would have all church bells ring for five minutes at 5 P.M. on Fridays to commemorate the weekend renewal of the spirit; would record surrounding streams and play these back in the town square.
>
> The Curator of Sight would commission fountains for all town squares; take rubbings of manhole covers for neighborhood displays; mount exhibitions of wrought iron cornices; would view the city as a stage and hire lighting designers to illuminate it.
>
> ...The Town Fool of Vancouver has been subsidized by the Canada Arts Council. He dresses up in a jester's costume and attends the city council sessions.
>
> Afterwards, he sits on the city hall steps reciting doggerel verses on the vagaries of the day's decisions...jesters share a common and invaluable trait: they are laughing with us, not at us, knowing that all human beings are gently askew.[42]

Why not hire someone who will help us all get a little more pleasure out of the simple things in life, who will poke a little fun so that we don't take ourselves too seriously? Songbirds and city sculpture and town fools are possible if we make them possible. Burgard's policies are just one example of creative work that has a positive and unifying influence on our world.

I'd like to close not with a focus on your needs and growth as an individual, but on the needs of our world for your creative talent. As creators we do more than create our own lives—we create the world we live in. We are shaped by our culture and shape it in turn, because our creative acts affect others, and we are part of a larger whole. The danger here is that we won't take action because we are waiting for someone else to take care of our community problems for us.

The human tendency to wait for others to take care of us reminds me of a tragic story. On March 27, 1977 at Tenerife Airport in the Canary Islands, an incoming plane struck a plane full of passengers waiting on the runway. In the chaos and confusion that ensued, many people remained in their seats, presumably waiting for flight attendants or other authorities to come and tell them what to do. A few passengers took matters into their own hands, clambering over tops of seats and jumping off the wing. Some broke bones in the fall, but they lived. Those who waited in their seats perished in flames that soon engulfed the plane.

In some ways our world is like that plane on the runway at Tenerife. We are faced with grave problems that require creative solutions, and we wait for someone else to help us at our peril. Participate! Don't let yourself project your responsibility onto someone else, such as a professional artist or an already established hero. Creative activities are not just for established professionals.

"We have to take life—society and human relations—more or less as we find them. The only thing that we can really make is our work. And deliberate work of the mind, imagination and hand, done, as Nietzsche said, 'notwithstanding,' in the long run remakes the world."

—EDMUND WILSON

Not only in our personal lives, but for our culture, we can offer the spiritual. Artistic work is spiritual, a personal meditation that provides food for the soul of others. Creative work connects us to what is fundamental and enduring and eternal. One of the things I appreciate most about art is its transcendent quality, its ability to raise consciousness to a higher level. After I encounter a work of art my vision is cleared. The small troubles over which I had felt peevish and upset no longer seem so important. My consciousness has been raised, and I am grateful.

> *"The most important function of art and science is to awaken the cosmic religious feeling and keep it alive."*
>
> —ALBERT EINSTEIN

There is something spiritual in the act of bringing things together, making them whole. And we always need to bring things together because humans tend to divide, to label, to distort. We can't help but perceive through filters and biases. I was reminded of this time and time again when I was nursing my infant son. I would look into his eyes and see my face reflected there and immediately think, "I look awful." And then I would realize that of course I didn't look awful to him. He had no conception of beauty. He had not yet learned to think, "Mama's got nice eyes, but her skin is blotchy." And then I would realize that I looked just like what I was—a person with many nights of broken sleep and no time to wash her hair.

Astronauts have a similar shift in perspective when they look at our planet from space. Mike Collins of Apollo 11 said, "The earth is one unit. You don't have the feeling that it's a fragmented place, that it's divided up into countries. You can't see any people, you can't hear any noise. It just seems like a very small, fragile, serene little sphere. It makes you wish that it really were as serene as it appears. It makes you wonder what any of us might do to make it a happier and more peaceful place."[43]

As Joseph Campbell says, our culture needs new myths, a new vision of what could be. As creative people, we can provide a new vision. We can, to paraphrase writer Hannah Arendt, make tangible the intangibility of things. The conventional world may deny unpleasant old realities and ignore uncomfortable new possibilities, but we can communicate them, even if we are not always appreciated for our effort.

"Vision is the art of seeing things invisible."

—Jonathan Swift

The conventional world may believe that if they can't see it, it's not there. It is our job to help them see. As artists we can shift the perspective of our world. We can help others see or hear or feel afresh. Locally and globally we can reunite what has been forced apart by old ways of thinking that have become destructive. Ours is not an easy role, because it requires taking risks, meeting opposition, and perhaps not earning financial rewards equal to our contribution. But our role is vital to our world. We can all make meaningful contributions, each in our own way.

And now we have come to the end of our journey together. Ahead of us lies nameless, faceless, formless reality—a jumble of chaotic information waiting for you to give it form and meaning. I'll say goodbye to you here. I expect that you will continue on your adventure, struggling with worthy problems and emerging a stronger person than when you began. Send me a postcard and let me know what you discover. Better yet, construct your own maps of the territory and share them with us all.

137

216 Jobs for Creative and Unconventional People

〜〜〜〜〜〜〜〜〜〜〜〜〜〜〜〜〜〜〜〜〜〜〜〜〜〜〜〜

Trail 1: Ideas

Writers

Arranger *(AEI)*
Arrangers transcribe musical compositions, adapting, reworking, and arranging them to accommodate different musical styles. They select voice, rhythm, tempo, instrument, and other features of a song. Arrangers are hired by the recording industry, music directors for TV and film, music publishers, music services, print-music licensees, theater groups, and performing artists. Arrangers usually freelance and are sometimes paid royalties, earning an annual income that ranges from less than $10,000 to over $100,000.

Biographer *(ASE)*
Biographers specialize in writing historical reconstructions of the lives of individuals. They base their narrative on a variety of biographical sources, such as diaries, letters, news articles, and interviews with relatives and other acquaintances. In their portrayal of their subject's life story, biographers attend to both a psychological analysis of character as well as the influence of historical events. Biographers are hired by celebrities and wealthy families and by publishers of books and magazines.

Columnist/Commentator *(EAS)*
Columnists write columns for magazines and newspapers; commentators write commentary which is taped or presented live on TV or radio. These writers gather, analyze, and interpret information to develop a personal perspective on their subject matter. They may specialize in a particular

field such as politics, health, sports, or gardening. Columnists are employed at newspapers, magazines, radio and TV stations. Their salaries range from $15,000 to $55,000, with top columnists making over $200,000 a year.

Composer *(ASE)*

Composers write original musical compositions such as operas, symphonies, and popular songs. They also transcribe their ideas into musical notation, sometimes using a computer to help them compose and edit their work. Composers work for record companies, recording groups, performing artists, production companies, and producers of opera and theatrical musical plays. They may also write music for radio, TV, and film.

Continuity Writer *(AES)*

Continuity writers write original scripts for TV or radio stations. Their scripts are read by an announcer to introduce, connect, and conclude the different parts of TV or radio programs, such as sports programs, nature shows, and musical events.

Copywriter *(ASI)*

Copywriters develop original ideas for advertising campaigns, writing the text of advertisements that appear in print media and scripts for broadcast media, as well as mail-order and other catalogs. While developing their approach, copywriters research the product or service they are advertising. They also consult with their clients and perhaps review marketing trends for comparable products or services. Copywriters are employed by advertising agencies, direct marketing agencies, and in-house advertising departments at large companies and corporations. An increasing number are self-employed. Typical salary ranges from $36,000 to $72,000.

Critic *(AES)*

Critics write reviews of artistic, literary, and musical events for print and broadcast media. They analyze the work, compare it to other works and evaluate it against objective standards, basing their opinions on knowledge, personal experience, and judgment. They may specialize in art, books, drama, movies, or music. Critics are employed at newspapers, magazines, radio and TV stations. Their salary ranges from $15,000 to over $55,000.

Crossword-Puzzle Maker *(ASE)*

Crossword-puzzle makers create crossword puzzles, including numbered lists of short definitions and completed puzzles that show the correct solution. After drawing and designing numbered blank squares, they choose words to fit the open spaces so that the spelling coincides both horizontally and vertically. Crossword-puzzle makers are hired by publishers of newspapers, magazines, and books.

Editorial Writer *(AES)*

Editorial writers examine the issues and topics that are generated by news events. Combining their views with the official position of their publication, they write editorials to influence public opinion. They may help determine the editorial position of their publication or decide on the contents of the editorial page. Some specialize in a particular area such as politics, international affairs, or financial matters. Editorial writers are employed by newspapers and news services. Their salaries range from $17,000 to over $55,000.

Humorist *(ASE)*

Humorists write amusing material for performers. They may be given a topic or select one themselves; they then write and revise the material until it meets their clients' approval. Some specialize in writing comedy shows or comedy routines for entertainers. Humorists may work for radio and TV shows. Many are self-employed.

Librettist *(ASE)*

Librettists write dialogue to accompany lengthy musical works that have been composed by someone else. They develop a dramatic story, adapting their text to fit the needs of composers and singers. Librettists are hired by producers and earn a salary that ranges from $10,000 to more than $50,000 per opera or musical.

Lyricist *(ASE)*

Lyricists write lyrics to accompany a melody written by someone else. They may be employed by performing artists, producers, record companies, recording groups, or advertising agencies.

Orchestrator *(AEI)*

Orchestrators transpose an existing musical score so that it better accommodates the abilities of particular instrumental and vocal musicians. Orchestrators are hired by producers of plays, movies, and TV shows. They also work for orchestras, bands, choral groups, arrangers, and individual musicians.

Playwright *(ASE)*

Playwrights write scripts for plays that are usually intended to be performed on stage. They write dialogue and describe action to be taken on stage and then revise the script during the time it is being rehearsed and prepared for production. Playwrights are employed by theater groups and producers of TV, radio, and motion pictures. They also sell their work to publishers.

Poet *(AES)*

Poets write poetry, of course; most of them earning little or nothing for their work. Poets sell their work to publishers of books, greeting cards, and magazines, including literary and academic journals. Magazines pay from $1.00 to $10.00 per line; greeting card publishers pay $15 to $80 per verse.

Reader *(AES)*

A reader reads plays, stories, novels, and screenplays and writes a synopsis to be reviewed by the producer or editorial staff. Once dramatic material is chosen for development, readers may recommend possible treatments. Readers may read foreign languages. They work for film and TV studios, associate producers, and independent movie production companies.

Reporter *(ASI)*

Reporters gather and analyze information about news events and write stories for print or broadcast media. They research the news, verify the accuracy of their information, organize and focus the material, and write a story following editorial standards. Radio reporters may read their story on the air. TV reporters may also direct a film crew, appear on TV, and give live reports at the site of breaking news. Reporters are employed by newspapers and radio and TV stations. Their salaries range from $11,000 to over $50,000.

Screenwriter *(AEI)*

Screenwriters write scripts and screenplays for video, radio, and film. After researching their topics, they may write an outline and summary before writing the entire script. They consult with the producer and director as they develop and revise the script. Screenwriters may collaborate with other writers and may adapt material from other genres. Screenwriters are hired by TV networks, radio stations, film studios, or corporate media centers; many freelance. Individual screenplays earn anywhere from $9,000 to more than $100,000.

Writer, Prose, Fiction and Nonfiction *(AIE)*

Writers write original prose. They research a topic that they have selected or had assigned, organize their material, and develop and focus their ideas as they write and revise. Writers of nonfiction may specialize in a certain field; writers of fiction in a certain genre, such as short stories or romance novels.

Writers are employed by industry, business, educational institutions, consulting firms, and government agencies. They often freelance to special and general interest magazines, book publishers, and advertising and public relations agencies. An Author's Guild survey reports that five percent of authors are able to support themselves through writing. Staff writers for journals and business organizations average $35,500, with a salary range from $28,000 to $41,000. Freelancers make $10 to $100 per hour and from $200 to $800 per day.

Directors

Artist and Repertoire Manager *(AES)*

A & R managers choose performing artists and musical compositions to be produced on phonograph records or compact discs. Based on their knowledge of public taste, popular music, and performing techniques, they audition and select the most appropriate performers and pieces. Some managers direct recording sessions and promote CD sales. A & R people work for recording studios, record companies, and radio stations. Some are self-employed.

Bureau Chief *(AES)*

Bureau chiefs work for newspapers or press syndicates in foreign countries or distant locations, such as remote suburbs or state capitals. They direct the work of people who gather and edit news stories and photos to be transmitted back to the home office. Bureau chiefs may need to translate news dispatches into English. They may also do some reporting.

Choral Director *(AES)*

Choral directors conduct groups of singers, such as church choirs and glee clubs. After auditioning members and choosing music that fits both the occasion and ability of the group, they direct them during rehearsals and performances. Some choral directors are involved in planning tours, scheduling performances, and arranging for group travel. Choral directors are hired by religious and educational institutions, such as churches and universities, and by musical groups, such as symphonies and choirs. They may hold several part-time jobs.

Creative Director *(AES)*

Creative directors develop the basic presentation for an advertisement, coordinating the work of the creative staff who write the copy and lay-out the design. After reviewing the information given by the client and discussing different options, they meet with heads of art, copywriting, and production departments to outline the basic concept, set a schedule, and attend to other client needs. Later they approve the promotional material that has been developed by the staff and present the final package to the client. Creative directors work for advertising agencies, direct marketing agencies, corporate advertising departments, and large media companies serving newspapers, magazines, and radio and TV stations.

Conductor, Orchestra *(AES)*

Orchestra conductors conduct groups of instrumental musicians. After auditioning members and positioning them to achieve balance, they choose a repertoire that fits the occasion and the talents of the group and then direct them during rehearsal and performance. Some orchestra conductors organize tours, schedule performances, and arrange for group travel and accommodations.

Orchestra conductors work for dance bands, symphony orchestras, opera or ballet companies, chamber ensembles, community orchestras, youth orchestras, and conservatories or schools with strong music departments. Salaries range on a per service basis from $50 to $300 and on a yearly basis from $12,000 to over $250,000.

Director, Music *(AES)*

Music directors conduct the orchestra during a recording or broadcast and direct the people who work in a studio music department. They choose music to suit the movie or TV show planned, perhaps hiring a composer to write a score. After auditioning and hiring musicians and other orchestra personnel, they assign tasks to their staff, such as scoring, arranging, and writing lyrics. Later they review progress. Music directors are hired by TV and motion picture producers.

145

Director, Stage *(AES)*

Stage directors direct an acting cast and technical crew, bringing to life their interpretation of a script or play. They rehearse the cast and guide actors and actresses to an opening performance consistent with their vision; they also coordinate other creative parts of the production, such as music, choreography, lighting, scenery, and costume design. Some directors audition and hire the cast.

Stage directors work in regional theaters, dinner theaters, repertory companies, and stock companies. Their salaries vary, depending on the kind of theater in which they work. For a five-week rehearsal period on Broadway, a stage director may make $36,750; for a four-week rehearsal period in a regional theater, from $3,415 to $13,595; and for a week of dinner theater or summer stock rehearsal, from $685 to $1,311.

Editor, Book *(AES)*

Book editors acquire manuscripts, edit them, and guide them through the production process. They read submissions, recommend acquisition based on what they anticipate to be market demand, and negotiate terms of agreement. Editors may supervise an editorial staff and develop ideas for books. They contribute ideas to authors and coordinate activities of the design, production, and publicity departments. Book editors are employed by publishing houses. They often work freelance on various aspects of the editorial process, such as acquisitions or (particularly) copy-editing. Their salaries range from under $22,000 to over $58,000.

Editor, Greeting Card *(AES)*

Greeting card editors choose and edit material for greeting card publishers. They read and evaluate original submissions from writers according to market trends and edit them according to the standards of their organization. They may coordinate the activities of those who design and print cards, and sometimes write and design cards as well.

Editor, News *(AES)*

News editors work for newspapers, planning the layout of each edition. They decide where stories should be placed, balancing each story's significance with space constraints and layout principles. They discuss placement of developing stories with other newspaper staff members. Working with news copy, photographs, and dummy layouts that indicate advertising space, they mark sheets to show the position of each story and photograph. News editors may also edit copy and write or revise headlines.

Performers

Actor *(AES)*

Actors and actresses interpret the words of a character in a script. After reading and rehearsing the script, they entertain an audience with their portrayal of their role, creating character through gestures, facial expressions, props, and so forth. So-called "triple threat" actors can also sing and dance. Actors and actresses may work on the stage, in professional regional theaters, dinner theaters, stock companies, and repertory companies. Network entertainment centers and local TV stations provide employment opportunities in TV. Motion pictures, industrial films, radio, night clubs, and advertising agencies also employ actors and actresses.

In 1993, the minimum weekly salary for union actors and actresses was $340 in off-Broadway theaters, $950 for Broadway stage productions, and $1,685 for film and TV speaking parts. Because employment is so irregular, the average yearly income from acting in the early '90s was $1,400 for screen actors and $5,200 for stage actors.

Clown *(EAC)*

Dressed in costumes and makeup, clowns entertain audiences by performing original routines or stock slapstick bits, using such skills as juggling, pantomime, walking on stilts, riding a unicycle, or creating balloon sculptures. Most clowns are employed by circus producers, but self-employed clowns find work through entertainment agencies and event-planning services. They also freelance at birthday parties and banquets. The average weekly salary for circus clowns was $200 in 1988.

Comedian *(AES)*

Comedians amuse their audiences by singing, dancing, telling jokes, or making funny faces. Comedians find work through talent agencies, entertainment agencies, TV producers, and owners or managers of comedy clubs, nightclubs, hotels, lounges, and cruise ships.

Dancer *(AER)*

Dancers may specialize in one style of dancing, such as ballet, tap, ballroom, folk, jazz, or modern. They are employed by dance companies and producers of TV shows and commercials, music videos, movies, musical comedy, and opera. Dancers also work in night clubs, hotels, resorts, and industrial exhibitions. Employment in dance tends to be very irregular. In 1993-94, dancers performing for union motion pictures made $99 minimum per day, and dancers performing in ballet and modern productions made a $587 minimum weekly salary.

Impersonator *(AES)*

Impersonators imitate people, animals, or inanimate objects. They entertain an audience by mimicking the voice, sound, physical form, expression, or mannerisms of their subject. Impersonators find work through night clubs, talent agencies, entertainment agencies, and TV producers.

Mime *(AEI)*

Mimes entertain an audience through pantomime. Using only body movements, gestures, and facial expressions, they portray tragic and comic moods and dramatic situations. Mimes freelance, finding work through entertainment agencies and event-planning services.

Singer *(AES)*

Singers are often classified according to the range of their voice, such as soprano or tenor, and may specialize in singing a particular type of music, such as opera, folk, rock, religious, or country and western. Singers are hired by managers of nightclubs and lounges and by producers of musical entertainment, such as operas, musicals, dinner theaters, regional theaters, variety shows, and recording studios. Many singers who never make it as solo artists find steady work, if not fame, as back-up acts and doing studio work for better-known recording artists.

Ventriloquist *(AES)*

Ventriloquists manipulate a dummy or puppet so that it appears to be alive and project their voices so that it appears to talk. They may also create the dummy and write the script for their performance. They find work through entertainment agencies and event-planning services.

Investigators

Biologist *(IAR)*

While this may not seem like a classically "artistic" field, creativity and innovation is important to a biologist's success. Biologists study plants and animals and how they relate to their environment. Some biologists do research in the field, meaning anything from tropical rainforests to alpine tundra. Others work in research laboratories with sophisticated technical equipment. Biologists may specialize in areas such as botany, zoology, ecology, or neuroscience. Many biologists hold faculty positions in colleges or universities. Others are employed by hospitals, research laboratories, the government, and the pharmaceutical industry. Median earnings for biologists in 1992 were $34,500, with the bottom ten percent earning less than $20,400 and the top ten percent earning more than $56,900.

Economist *(IAS)*

Successful economists are creative wizards when it comes to finding and solving problems. They collect and analyze data, then develop forecasts, prepare reports, formulate recommendations, and advise clients. Many economists apply economic principles to data in a particular area, such as agriculture, health, labor, the environment, or international trade.

Economists work for banks, government agencies, economic research firms, management consulting firms, securities and commodities brokers, computer and data-processing companies, and colleges and universities.

In 1993, salaries of economists with the Federal Government averaged about $53,500. In 1992, the median base salary of business economists, most of whom held advanced degrees, was $65,000.

Experimental Psychologist *(IAE)*
Experimental psychologists must be creative in the way they structure experiments and, particularly, interpret unusual data. They formulate hypotheses and design experiments to investigate problems in areas such as motivation, memory, learning, or substance use. After observing and recording behavioral data (using human or animal subjects), they analyze its significance with statistical techniques and then write up their interpretation of the results.

149

Experimental psychologists are employed by colleges and universities, government agencies, research organizations, ergonomics industries, and consulting firms. The median salary for Ph.D. psychologists in research positions in 1991 was $50,000. Median salaries in university psychology departments were $32,000 for assistant professors and $55,000 for full professors.

Social Psychologist *(IAE)*
Social psychologists investigate human behavior in a social environment, attempting through research to understand and predict the behavior of individuals in groups. The groups studied might be racial, religious, political, or occupational in nature; the research might focus on such topics as leadership, group dynamics, or romantic attraction. Following research design and statistical principles, social psychologists design experimental observations, interviews, or questionnaires, collect and analyze data, and then write a report on their findings.

Social psychologists work in universities, colleges, marketing research firms, management consulting firms, and government agencies. A 1991 survey indicated that the median annual salary of doctoral-level psychologists holding research positions was $50,000. In university psychology departments, the median salaries ranged from $32,000 for assistant professors to $55,000 for full professors.

Coordinators

Account Executive *(AES)*

Account executives work in advertising agencies, coordinating advertising campaigns for their clients. After learning from their client about the products or services to be advertised, they draw on their knowledge of the media and the target audience and consult with agency staff to develop an advertising approach and estimate a budget. The account executive then submits the plan and budget to the client, and if it's approved, directs the work of copywriters, layout artists, market researchers, and others who carry out the campaign.

Contestant Coordinator *(AES)*

Contestant coordinators work for producers of TV game shows, coordinating that part of studio work that involves contestants. They provide information to people who would like to be contestants, screen and file applications, call back applicants to arrange a mock game for the producer, and notify those applicants who are selected to participate. Some contestant coordinators interview and select contestants. Once contestants have been selected, coordinators brief them on the rules and procedures for the show and attend to their needs in the studio.

Department Head, College or University *(EAI)*

Department heads work in junior colleges, colleges, and universities, administering the affairs of their department. They schedule classes, assign instructors, and recruit and interview applicants for faculty and staff positions. They prepare the budget, teach in the department, and perform a variety of administrative tasks.

Director of Vital Statistics *(EAI)*

Directors of vital statistics need a creative bent in order to best evaluate information and come up with innovative solutions. They conduct special statistical studies and direct the activities of subordinates who collect, record, and tabulate statistics on events such as births, deaths, marriages, and diseases. They also develop methods for registering or certifying births and deaths and other events throughout the state. Directors of vital statistics are employed by state governments.

Director, Classification and Treatment *(AES)*

Classification and treatment directors work in prisons and other correctional institutions, planning, coordinating, and directing rehabilitation programs. Following established guidelines, they provide for the emotional, physical, social, and spiritual needs of inmates. After administering psychological tests and reviewing case reports, they assess an inmate's potential for rehabilitation and recommend a disposition, such as parole, transfer, treatment, or training. They also give speeches to educate the public.

≈≈≈

Director, Instructional Material *(ASE)*

Instructional material directors work for public school districts, coordinating the development and use of educational material. They direct workers who maintain and distribute educational materials for the school system. After reviewing educational materials such as textbooks and videotapes, they recommend the purchase of new material, implement its use in the schools, and train teachers to use new technology. They also help staff develop their own instructional materials.

Director, Program *(AES)*

Program directors select and schedule the programming broadcast by their TV stations. To provide a balanced mix of programs that will attract a large audience and high ratings, they consult with marketers, study demographics, and watch programs on competitive stations. Following FCC regulations, they choose film packages, syndicated shows, reruns, and locally produced programs, scheduling them with public service announcements, station breaks, and commercials. They also purchase programs and follow a budget.

Program directors are employed by independent commercial stations, network-affiliated stations, and public TV stations. In 1985, salaries for program directors ranged from $15,000 to more than $90,000, with most in the $25,000 to $50,000 range.

Director, State-Assessed Properties *(AEI)*

This is another one of those jobs that doesn't seem creative right off the bat, but does require (or at least benefit from) the ability to creatively gather and assess information. Directors of state-assessed properties coordinate a property assessment program that is designed to equalize tax rates once property values change. They send appraisers out to inspect properties and interview owners, analyze the data gathered, prepare reports, recommend changes in taxation, and allocate revenue among districts. They also represent the tax commission in various meetings. They work for local or state governments.

Location Manager *(EAR)*

Location managers find and get permits to use property for movies or TV shows. After learning from the director about the kinds of background needed for outdoor scenes, they search established files and seek out new locations. Once a suitable location is found, they negotiate to use the property and obtain permission to film on site. They may hire extras and arrange for transportation of the crew. Location managers are hired by producers and production managers of motion pictures and television shows.

Manager, Forms Analysis *(EAS)*

While this job may not sound particularly creative, it requires one to analyze information and come up with creative solutions. Forms analysis managers coordinate analysis of various sorts of business forms, including improving their format and design, increasing content effectiveness, and reducing production costs. Forms analysis managers are employed by large companies and federal, state, and county governments.

Manager, Records Analysis *(EAI)*

This is another one of those jobs that doesn't seem creative right off the bat, but does require (or at least benefit from) the ability to creatively analyze information and generate new, improved procedures. Records analysis managers coordinate an organization's record-keeping staff, as well as working to simplify filing systems, protect important records, and reduce waste. Records analysis managers are employed by large companies and county, state, and federal governments.

Manager, Reports Analysis *(EAS)*

Yet another job that may not sound creative, but does involve creatively analizing information in order to create innovative new solutions. Reports analysis managers plan new report formats, coordinating the work of people who analyze existing reports for cost effectiveness. They evaluate the recommendations of their staff and approve changes. Reports analysis managers are employed by large companies and federal, state, and county government.

Music Supervisor *(EAS)*

Music supervisors work for the public schools, directing teachers of vocal and instrumental music and, with the help of teachers and administrators, developing a curriculum for music education. In order to improve classroom instruction, they observe and evaluate both teaching methods and teaching materials. They also order training supplies and equipment, authorize the purchase and repair of musical instruments, and organize musical groups to represent the schools at community events.

153

Program Coordinator *(AES)*

Program coordinators work in amusement parks that feature performing animals, coordinating the contribution of the educational department. After gathering educational information and verifying the format of the performance with the animal trainer, they write or review a script to accompany the show. They also prepare brochures, greet visitors, and answer questions. Some program coordinators memorize the script and speak during the performance.

Sight-Effects Specialist *(AES)*

Sight-effects specialists provide stage lighting and scenic effects for theatrical productions and direct the electrical crew that installs and arranges that lighting. In order to set the mood and determine how the stage should be lighted, they study working drawings of the set, read the continuity script and confer with people who produce the show. They order any special contraptions necessary to achieve scenic effects, and sometimes handle back projections. Sight-effects specialists work at colleges and universities and at theaters of all sizes. They may also work for rock bands, performance artists, and dance troupes, among other types of performers.

Traffic-Safety Administrator *(AER)*

This is another one of those jobs that doesn't seem creative right off the bat, but does require (or at least benefit from) the ability to creatively gather and assess information. Traffic-safety administrators work for municipal governments, planning and directing traffic-safety programs. They examine the patterns of traffic accidents to figure out where improvements need to be made and coordinate the activities of volunteer groups dedicated to traffic safety. They also test employees to determine their driving ability and attitude.

Evaluators

Appraiser, Art *(IAS)*

Art appraisers evaluate works of art to determine their authenticity and assess their value. When judging the authenticity of an art object, they rely on their knowledge of art history, including materials and techniques employed by different artists. They examine antiques and paintings and other art objects to verify their creators and their historical periods. In order to detect forgeries, they may x-ray or illuminate art works or perform chemical tests. Art appraisers usually freelance their services to art museums, auction houses, corporations, and individuals who collect, insure, buy or sell art. Large museums and auction houses may have appraisers on staff.

Bar Examiner *(AES)*

This is a job that, while not conventionally "artistic," requires creative use of writing and analysis skills. Bar examiners work for state bar associations, testing candidates who wish to practice the law. Using the legal code in their jurisdiction, they prepare a written examination that requires candidates to demonstrate their knowledge of the law. After the examinations are completed, bar examiners evaluate candidate performance against accepted standards, announce the names of those who pass, submit them to an oral examination, and recommend that they be permitted to practice law.

Cryptanalyst *(AIE)*

Cryptanalysts decode secret messages for military, political, or law enforcement agencies. They use a variety of techniques to break the code, including computers and even chemical analysis, then attempt to corroborate the decoded message against other printed sources.

Field Representative *(EAS)*

The creative aspect of this job comes in its relative freedom of movement, as well as the opportunity to work creatively with information and people. Field representatives work for business services and wholesalers, making franchise operations more efficient. To this end they oversee the work of dealers and distributors and provide advice on policies and procedures. They determine the feasibility of establishing new dealerships and distributorships. Once a franchise is up and running they evaluate its effectiveness, planning modifications and expansions.

Graphologist *(ACS)*

Graphologists analyze handwriting in order to evaluate personality. From a sample of handwriting they observe both overall appearance and minute detail, measuring letter height and slant, perusing unusual features with a magnifying glass or microscope. They interpret their personality findings according to principles of handwriting analysis. Graphologists consult to business and industry, using their skills in a variety of ways: screening job applicants, eliminating criminal suspects, examining questioned documents, and helping identify patients and students with emotional troubles. They may also use their skills to entertain.

Intelligence Research Specialist *(AEI)*

Intelligence research specialists direct research designed to determine the feasibility of different military strategies. After talking with military leaders and other support staff to better understand the problem and proposed solutions, they use research techniques and computer analyses to predict the probable success of each strategy. Then they evaluate their research results before recommending or discouraging particular strategies. Intelligence research specialists are employed not only by the military, but by other government agencies as well.

Intelligence Specialist *(AES)*

Intelligence specialists analyze information on subversive activities in foreign countries. Drawing on their knowledge of an area's culture, geography, economy, and political structure, they evaluate military activities, political conditions, and enemy propaganda, in order to facilitate counteraction by the United States. Intelligence specialists work for the CIA, the military, and other government agencies.

Patent Agent *(AEI)*

Patent agents prepare patent applications and present them in patent courts and the U.S. Patent Office. They must be registered with the U.S. Patent Office, and cannot present cases in other courts. Patent agents are employed by law firms, universities, any corporation with a patent or intellectual property department, businesses that plan, acquire or license products, and any private individual who needs to prepare and prosecute a patent application.

Promoters

Auctioneer *(AES)*

Auctioneers work at auction houses or for auction services, selling merchandise such as artwork, cars, machinery, furniture, or livestock. After appraising and sorting the merchandise, they select an article and either give or ask for a starting bid. To encourage buyers and stimulate bidding, they describe the article, perhaps providing information about its previous history, and later close the sale to the highest bidder.

Fashion Coordinator *(EAS)*

Fashion coordinators organize activities that are designed to promote new fashions. They gain information on developing trends by attending fashion shows, studying journals, and visiting garment centers. They consult with buyers to learn what merchandisers plan to purchase, then choose articles to be worn at fashion shows, providing information on current fashion and the use of accessories. Fashion coordinators are employed by retail stores, buying offices, pattern companies, and apparel manufacturers.

Public-Relations Representative *(EAS)*

Public-relations (PR) representatives provide information about their employer through such strategies as audio-visual presentations, annual reports, news releases, fact sheets, convention exhibits, and speaking tours. They maintain cooperative relationships with representatives from the media and various public groups. They also seek to understand the attitudes and concerns of their clients' customers and employees.

Public relations representatives work for a wide variety of employers, including individuals, businesses, special interest groups, nonprofit organizations and health care organizations, social service and government agencies, educational and financial institutions, and manufacturing firms, as well as for independent PR firms. In 1992, salaries for PR reps ranged from under $20,000 to over $60,000. The median annual salary for those working full-time was about $32,000; for specialists, including managers, it was about $44,000.

Sales-Service Promoter *(AES)*

Sales-service promoters work for any industry, promoting the products or services of their firm. To increase sales and create goodwill, they prepare displays, call on merchants, tour the country, and give speeches at conventions. Some sales-service promoters demonstrate new technological products.

Collections Organizers

Acquisitions Librarian *(SAI)*

Acquisitions librarians choose and order books and periodicals and other materials for a given library. After perusing publisher's catalogs and making sure that their preliminary choices do not duplicate those already in the collection, they list publications for purchase and circulate the list within the library for review. They also analyze information on cost and delivery dates to select the best vendor. Acquisitions librarians work in public libraries, academic libraries, special libraries, and government or corporation libraries. The average salary for experienced special librarians in 1992 was $31,800.

Archivist *(AES)*

Archivists appraise, exhibit, and store documents of historical value. They analyze documents to determine their value to posterity, direct the description, cataloging, and cross-indexing of archival material, and select and edit documents for publication or exhibition. Archivists may specialize in an area of history or technology, or specialize in the type of documents they archive. Archivists are employed by the federal, state, and local government; corporations; libraries; museums; historical societies; educational institutions; religious, fraternal, and conservation organizations, and professional associations. Salaries range from $17,000 to $50,000.

Audiovisual Librarian *(EAS)*

Audiovisual librarians administer a library of audiovisual materials, such as films, tapes, cassettes, and framed art prints. They plan audiovisual programs and may lead discussion after presentations. After contacting distributors of audiovisual materials, they evaluate and purchase materials, summarize new acquisitions for the catalog, and then help patrons and other library personnel select materials. They may operate audiovisual equipment themselves or train others to operate and maintain it.

≋
158

Audiovisual librarians are employed in academic libraries, public libraries, special libraries, and school library/media centers. They may also work in information centers or libraries that are part of the government, corporations, advertising agencies, museums, medical centers, and professional associations. In 1993, experienced librarians earned an average of $37,900 in the public schools and $44,500 with the federal government.

Young-Adult Librarian *(AES)*

Young-adult librarians provide special services designed to stimulate the reading and communication skills of young adults. They acquire books and materials especially suitable for young adults, compile a list of interesting library materials, give talks, and help their patrons make selections. After conferring with parents, teachers, and community leaders, they plan and conduct programs and activities, such as creative writing clubs, photography contests, and film series. Young-adult librarians are most likely to work in public libraries and school library/media centers. In 1993, experienced school librarians earned an average salary of $37,900.

Trail 2: Ideas & People

Mentors

Clergy Member *(SAE)*

Clergy members include rabbis, Protestant ministers, and Roman Catholic priests. They conduct religious worship, provide spiritual guidance, and perform a variety of religious rites according to their faith. For example, they may interpret religious doctrine, write and deliver sermons, teach those who seek conversion, oversee educational programs, conduct weddings and funerals, visit the sick, and comfort the bereaved.

Many clergy members serve individual congregations. Others work in hospitals, educational institutions, correctional institutions, the military, and community service agencies. Estimated average compensation (which includes benefits) in 1992 was $38,000 to $60,000 for rabbis, $44,000 for ministers, and $29,000 for priests.

Counselor *(SAE)*

Counselors help individuals and groups to understand and cope with problems that may be personal, social, educational, or vocational in nature. They assess the nature of the client's concerns and facilitate personal growth and problem-solving in the context of a trusting relationship. They may refer clients to other agencies. Counselors may specialize in such areas as career, marriage and family, mental health, multicultural, and drug and alcohol.

159

Counselors are employed by educational institutions, correctional institutions, mental health centers, health care facilities, health maintenance organizations, and vocational rehabilitation centers. They may also be self-employed. Their salaries ranged from $18,000 to $50,000, with a median salary of $30,000 in 1992. School counselors had a median salary of $40,400.

Dance Therapist *(ASI)*

Dance therapists plan and lead dance and movement activities in order to improve the physical and mental health of patients. They lead individual and group dance sessions, adapting their programs as patients progress. Dance therapists are employed by schools, correctional facilities, independent expressive arts therapy centers, and a variety of health-care facilities, including hospitals, mental-health centers, nursing homes, and rehabilitation centers. Salaries range from $14,000 to over $50,000.

Marriage and Family Therapist *(SAE)*

Marriage and family therapists help individuals, couples, and families. They may focus on the marital relationship, a child's behavioral problems, or the concerns of blended or step-families. With a focus on resolving present problems, they explore family history or interactional patterns and make suggestions for change. Marriage and family therapists are employed by mental health centers, employee assistance programs, and health maintenance organizations. Some are self-employed in private practice and may consult to religious organizations and family businesses.

Music Therapist *(ASI)*

Music therapists use music and musical activities to improve the physical and emotional health of their patients. Working with other health-care professionals, they plan musical activities designed to help patients build confidence, increase social activity, and express feelings. They may teach songs, play musical instruments, and choose background music for their institution. Music therapists work at hospitals, nursing homes, extended-care facilities, correctional facilities, mental-health centers, rehabilitation centers, and expressive arts therapy centers. Salaries range from $13,000 to $38,000.

Speech Pathologist *(SAI)*

Speech pathologists diagnose and treat problems involving speech and language. After reviewing an individual's background, they use special instruments and a variety of tests to evaluate problems such as stuttering or slurred speech. Then they plan and implement a treatment program, teaching new skills, such as sign language, to their clients and monitoring their progress with audio-visual equipment.

Speech pathologists work in educational settings, home health care agencies, hospitals and doctor's offices, speech, language, and hearing centers, and in solo or group private practice. Median salary for full-time speech pathologists in 1992 was $36,000.

Negotiators

Commissioner, Conservation of Resources *(AES)*

This is a job that requires creative problem-solving and working with others to develop innovative solutions. Conservation of resources commissioners work for the state government to conserve natural resources and promote their use in the public interest, as well as presenting reports on these issues. These commissioners develop conservation programs and set limits on consumption. They negotiate with mining and drilling companies to observe standards and extract resources efficiently. In order to solve conservation problems related to economic development, they speak with representatives of government, labor, and industry.

Director, Council on Aging *(EAS)*

Another job that involves creative problem-solving, innovation, and creative exchange of information. It involves work in local and state government to solve problems of senior citizens. They plan research studies to learn more about problems such as health or employment, and then combat those problems with new policies and strategies, help set up local programs and services for the elderly, coordinate programs with other organizations, and promote their programs and the interests of the aged by delivering speeches, negotiating with community leaders, preparing educational materials for the public, and recommending changes in public policy and legislation.

161

Editor, Newspaper *(AES)*

Newspaper editors formulate editorial policies and direct the operation of a newspaper. They appoint heads to the advertising, circulation, and production departments, supervising their work. They negotiate with departmental heads and an editorial policy committee to develop policies and procedures for the paper. Newspaper editors also write editorials, review financial reports, and represent their paper at various functions.

Editor, Technical and Scientific Publications *(ASE)*

Editors for technical and scientific publications coordinate the work of writers who prepare material on specific fields, such as manufacturing or medical research. In order to develop a focus for their publication, they stay abreast of developments and analyze trends. They assign subjects to staff writers, supervise their work, and edit their drafts. Technical and scientific publications editors work in business and industry and for educational institutions, research organizations, nonprofit organizations, and the government. In 1992, the average salary for technical editors in the federal government was $40,669.

Supervisor, Historic Sites *(AES)*

Historic sites supervisors work in the state government directing people who acquire and preserve natural phenomena and historic sites, such as homes and battlefields. After negotiating with property owners, they authorize the acquisition and restoration of historic sites. These supervisors may help private individuals and civic groups acquire landmarks that aren't suitable for state support. Historic sites supervisors also direct archeological research in state parks and direct the preparation of museum exhibits and multimedia exhibits designed to encourage public attendance.

Instructors

Cantor *(ASE)*

Cantors lead the musical part of religious services. They chant or read religious texts during services, arranging music and leading the congregation in singing. They may compose their own music or variations on traditional church music. They may also lead the choir and teach singing or chanting to groups within the congregation. Cantors are employed by churches and other religious groups.

Choreographer *(AES)*

Choreographers compose original dances or new interpretations of traditional dance music. After studying the music and any script involved, they create dance routines and block the movements out on stage, adapting the choreography as needed once rehearsal begins. They may audition performers, choose dancers for the cast, and teach them the dance steps and routines during rehearsal. Choreographers may specialize in different dance forms, such as ballet, jazz, folk, or modern dance. Choreographers are hired, usually one show at a time, by producers of shows for theaters and nightclubs or by producers of shows for TV or film. Their salaries are quite variable, ranging from less than $750 a week to over $10,000 a week.

Dramatic Coach *(ASE)*

Dramatic coaches help actors and actresses improve their acting techniques. After evaluating a performer's ability, they teach dramatic skills such as script analysis, character interpretation, stage presence, cinematic technique, and voice projection. They may also help prepare a performer for a professional career and give advice on clothing, makeup, and auditions. They may specialize in stage or screen. Dramatic coaches may work independently or be employed by schools, colleges, universities, and theater groups. Those employed by educational institutions have salaries that range from $10,000 to $40,000, while self-employed coaches may make $60,000 or more.

Graduate Assistant *(SAE)*

While no one should really aspire to a *career* as a graduate assistant, per se, this is a good way to get a foot in the door in your chosen creative field. Graduate assistants help faculty in colleges and universities teach courses and do research. For example, graduate assistants may teach lower-level courses, grade papers and exams, facilitate discussion in study sections, do library or laboratory research, prepare data for statistical analysis, and write up research results. Graduate assistants are employed by colleges and universities, usually on a part-time basis while they are taking graduate courses.

Instructor, Dancing *(ASE)*

Dancing instructors plan lessons after observing their students' abilities and limitations. Explaining and demonstrating dancing styles, techniques and steps, they give feedback as students practice new skills. They may specialize in teaching one or more forms of dance, such as ballet, jazz, tap, modern, or ballroom dance. Dancing instructors are employed by private schools, educational institutions, and dance studios. Their fees range from $25 to $250 per hour. Self-employed dancing instructors may charge fees ranging from $10 to $100 per class.

Instructor, Modeling *(ASE)*

Modeling instructors teach students how to improve their appearance. After observing and analyzing physical characteristics such as figure, posture, and coloring, the instructor will explain and demonstrate ways to improve appearance. Incorporating principles of modeling, they will teach students how to apply makeup, how to walk and climb stairs, and how to select and coordinate clothing. Modeling instructors are employed by modeling schools and occasionally by modeling agencies.

Liberal Arts Faculty *(SAI)*

Liberal arts faculty work for universities, colleges, and community colleges, teaching liberal arts subjects such as fine arts, English literature, foreign languages, and film studies. They prepare and give lectures, facilitate discussion in seminars, give exams and grade papers, and advise students on their course of study. Liberal arts faculty often do original research in their fields, reading and writing scholarly articles or textbooks. Full-time associate professors in artistic fields make around $40,000.

Librarian *(SAI)*

Librarians help people access information from a collection of books, periodicals, documents, and other materials. They search catalog files and library shelves to find information for patrons and also teach patrons how to use reference sources. In addition to maintaining and displaying the library collection, they may also select, order, catalog, classify, and compile lists of library materials. Librarians may specialize in such areas as reference, outreach, or circulation.

Librarians work in academic libraries, public libraries, special libraries, and school library/media centers. Librarians may also work in libraries or information centers in the government, religious organizations, medical centers, research laboratories, corporations, law firms, advertising agencies, museums, nonprofit organizations, and professional associations. In 1993, salaries for experienced librarians in the public schools averaged $37,900; salaries for experienced librarians in the federal government, $44,500.

Teacher, Drama *(ASE)*

Drama teachers teach acting and other theater arts and may produce and direct plays. They evaluate the abilities and limitations of their students and plan instruction. Using lecture, demonstration, improvisation, and other exercises, they teach dramatic principles and techniques such as character development, dialect, movement, and projection. They may audition students, assign roles, direct rehearsals, and supervise nonperformance tasks such as constructing the set, operating the lights, designing the costumes, or applying stage makeup.

Drama teachers are usually employed by educational institutions. The salaries of teachers in public secondary schools averaged $33,700 in 1990-1991. Salaries for drama teachers at colleges and universities range from $17,000 to more than $50,000.

Teacher, Elementary School *(SAI)*

Elementary school teachers work in public and private schools teaching academic subjects, study skills, and rules of social conduct to their students. Sometimes they tutor individual students and meet with parents. Salaries for public school elementary school teachers in 1992-93 averaged about $34,800; teachers in private schools generally made less.

Teacher, Preschool *(SAE)*

Preschool teachers nurture and teach children under the age of five. In an informal and relatively unstructured setting, they care for the basic needs of small children while they help them learn through play. Organizing activities that will stimulate a child's growth, they see to it that each child has a daily balance of individual and group attention and time to play and rest. They also record each child's progress and discuss his or her development with parents. Preschool teachers are employed by families, daycare centers, preschools, religious and educational institutions, the government, businesses, and community agencies. Weekly earnings for full-time preschool teachers in 1992 averaged $260.

Teacher, Secondary School *(SAE)*

Secondary school teachers teach one or several subjects—such as English, foreign languages, social studies, speech, and human ecology—to junior high or high school students. They may also meet with parents, sponsor extracurricular activities, and counsel troubled students. Secondary school teachers are employed by public and private high schools and junior high schools. In the 1992-1993 school year, the average salary for public secondary school teachers was $36,000.

Trainer *(SAE)*

Trainers develop and conduct training programs for employees, which may include lectures, computer tutorials, storytelling sessions, and/or multimedia presentations. They conduct training sessions and later evaluate or test trainees to determine the effectiveness of their programs. Trainers may specialize in areas such as career development, writing skills, sales techniques, or cross-cultural aspects of foreign trade. Trainers are employed by corporations, businesses, government agencies, educational and medical institutions, and nonprofit organizations. Self-employed trainers may conduct seminars outside the workplace.

Supervisors

Editor, City *(AES)*

City editors work for newspapers, supervising staff who gather and report the news. They direct reporters and photographers to cover developing news events and other stories. They supervise editors, review edited copy, and allocate newspaper space. They may guide the newspaper on policy and position. Their salaries range from less than $16,000 to over $55,000.

Editor, Department *(AES)*

Department editors work for newspapers, supervising staff on a specialized section of a newspaper, such as sports, business, or entertainment. They select material, assign staff to write or photograph stories, determine content, edit copy, and supervise layout on their section. Department editors may write a regular column as well. Their salaries range from $15,000 to over $55,000.

Editor, Publications *(AES)*

Publications editors plan the contents of magazines and other publications and supervise their preparation. They write, rewrite, and edit manuscripts. They choose themes, assign articles to writers and assign pictures and illustrations to photographers and artists. Publications editors supervise subordinate editors, hire staff, negotiate with freelancers, and plan budgets and future issues. They oversee final production of the publication, including page layouts. Publications editors are employed by magazines and business and trade publishers. Their salaries range from $20,000 to over $100,000.

Production Manager, Advertising *(ASE)*

Advertising production managers supervise people who prepare advertisements, including designers, illustrators, photographers, paste-up artists, and typographers. Visual technical experts, they review proofs to be sure they meet specifications and coordinate workers to prepare final layouts on schedule. Before submitting final layouts for printing, they examine the layout proof and specify margin widths and color corrections. Advertising production managers work for advertising agencies, printing companies, and in-house corporate marketing departments.

Story Editor *(ASE)*

Story editors evaluate manuscripts and supervise writers who create scripts for TV and film. They evaluate a story's potential for development into a script and recommend the purchase of material. They hire and assign writers and then review and edit their work to prepare scripts for production. Story editors are employed at TV and film studios and at the larger independent film production companies.

Supervisor, Show Operations *(ASE)*

Show operations supervisors work at amusement parks and theme parks, supervising performers and technicians. With anticipated audience size in mind, they review and adjust the performance schedule and arrange shift assignments. They also answer questions and handle complaints from park guests.

Supervisor, Sign Shop *(EAS)*

Sign shop supervisors follow customer requests and assign workers to design signs and banners on computer. Once the computer has cut letters, they make sure specifications are followed as the letters are applied to the sign. Sign shop supervisors work for sign companies and sign departments of large corporations.

Persuaders

Note: Unlike the other listings in this appendix, the two sales descriptions represent an amalgam of several DOT listings. Thus, while I hope you find them useful, I wanted to warn you that you will not find them listed like this in any other reference work.

Sales Representative, Independent *(AES/EAS)*

Independent sales reps work in all sorts of fields, from those intimately associated with the arts (selling books, fine arts, graphics, dancing instructions, etc.) to the industrial and commercial. This job allows intimate contact with a number of creative fields as well as a flexibility in work hours and an unstructured work environment that many creative types find attractive. It is not uncommon to move from a sales job in a creative industry to more direct work in that field, assisted by the special knowledge of the market gained in sales.

Salesperson, Retail *(EAS/EAR)*

Like the independent sales rep, the in-house or in-store salesperson may be granted special access to a creative field (such as fine art, clothing, accessory, and floral design, book publishing, etc.) and flexible hours that suit their temperament. In addition, their sales knowledge may lead them to more direct work in that field. (Someone who has worked in a bookstore, for instance, might seem very attractive to a fiction publisher looking for employees with "real world" knowledge of their market, instead of just the generic English degree held by so many job-seekers.)

Wedding Consultant *(AES)*

Wedding consultants provide advice to couples on all aspects of planning a wedding. Not all wedding consultants provide the same services, but most offer some of the following: maintaining a gift register and selling wedding gifts; selling wedding gowns and making recommendations regarding the bridal trousseau and clothing for the bridal party;, shopping for the bride or helping her choose china, silverware, glassware, flowers, and so on; arranging for music and photography and a catering service; providing advice on etiquette during rehearsal. Wedding consultants are usually self-employed. Some work in bridal shops and large department stores.

Trail 3: Ideas & Things

Designers

Architect *(AIR)*

Architects plan and design buildings. The job requires knowledge of design, engineering, building materials, building codes, and construction methods, and the ability to come up with a plan to meet a particular client's needs. Once the plan is approved by the client, they prepare scale drawings and specifications and draw up building contracts. Architects may help their clients get bids and select contractors; periodically they may observe on-site construction to ensure that work proceeds according to plan. Specialties include commercial, residential, industrial, and institutional architecture.

Architects work for architecture firms, engineering firms, schools of architecture, builders, real estate developers, industrial organizations, the military, and government agencies. Median salary in 1992 for licensed architects who were not partners or principals was $36,700; median salary for firm partners or principals was $50,000; some partners earned more than $100,000.

Art Director *(AES)*

Art directors design and direct the construction of sets for motion pictures and television productions. After reading the script and conferring with the producer and director, they research appropriate architectural styles, estimate construction costs, present plans and estimates, and work within a budget. They coordinate the construction and decoration of the set to ensure that it follows design. Art directors also direct the production of graphics and animation. They are hired by TV and film directors and production designers.

≋

169

Bank-Note Designer *(AER)*

Bank-note designers design currency, stamps, bonds, and other securities for the U.S. and foreign governments. They modify original sketches as needed for technical constraints, draw new design elements to discourage counterfeiting, and select or suggest ink colors. They may originate new designs and get approval from the issuing agency.

Cloth Designer *(AER)*

Cloth designers create new designs for textiles, including rugs and woven fabrics. Combining their knowledge of textiles with information on fashion trends, they design new fabric, specifying such details as color, pattern, and finish. They sketch their designs and examine a sample of fabric to see if further modifications are needed. Cloth designers are employed by textile industries and carpet and rug manufacturers. Their salaries range from $12,000 to more than $50,000, with a median salary in 1990 of $26,000.

Clothes Designer *(ASR)*

Clothing designers create new fashion designs for men's, women's, and children's clothing and accessories. After analyzing fashion trends, they sketch drawings of their designs, possibly directing others to draw and cut the pattern and construct a sample garment. They examine the sample on a model and alter the design if necessary. Clothes designers may specialize according to the kind of clothes they design, such as sportswear, lingerie, handbags, or costumes.

Clothing designers are employed by clothing and pattern manufacturers, fashion salons, high fashion department stores, and specialty shops.

Some freelance, doing custom work for individuals. Costume designers work for theater companies, dance ensembles, and directors and producers of movies and TV shows. The salaries of clothing designers range from $12,000 to over $50,000, with a 1990 median of $26,000.

Color Expert *(AES)*

Color experts give advice on esthetic color combinations. They know what shades of color are fashionable and what psychological effects are produced by different colors, and they help their clients choose colors for interiors, fashions, and graphic arts. Color experts are hired by color associations, the fashion and textile industries, and by architectural, interior design, and graphic design firms.

Commercial Designer *(AER)*

Commercial designers work for manufacturers, designing graphics for manufactured goods such as wallpaper, china, toys, and tile. They study marketing trends and styles of ornamentation and then integrate that with their knowledge of design and any constraints presented by the materials. They create a design, submit it to the client or supervisor for feedback, and make changes as necessary.

Display Designer *(AES)*

Display designers design banners, flags, and other decorations for special occasions. After talking with clients about the celebration, theme, and budget, they sketch a design, select decorations at hand or construct new decorations, and may direct others to construct and set up decorations. Display artists design interior displays and window displays; outside display designers specialize in designing outdoor displays. Display designers are employed by graphic design firms, department stores, and display houses.

Displayer, Merchandise *(ARE)*

Merchandise displayers work in retail stores, displaying merchandise in windows and on sales floors. They design original displays or follow the manager's suggestions to attract customers to merchandise such as furniture or clothing or cooking equipment. Using hand tools and a variety of materials, they construct backgrounds and props on which they arrange merchandise and place signs. Some merchandise displayers are employed by display houses that produce displays for showrooms, trade shows, and special events.

Exhibit Designer *(ASE)*

Exhibit designers work for museums, designing both permanent and temporary exhibits and displays. They confer with museum administrators and staff to learn the exhibit's purpose, content, location, and budget. Then they plan the construction of the exhibit, preparing preliminary drawings and detailed construction diagrams. Exhibit designers submit the design for approval and adapt it as needed. They oversee construction and installation of the exhibit to ensure that it conforms to their specifications. After arranging for acquisition of objects, they oversee their placement in the exhibit, along with accompanying information.

Floral Designer *(RAE)*

Floral designers work for florists, selecting and arranging flowers and other foliage according to customer request. They talk with the customer about the occasion, the kind of arrangement desired, and price and delivery details. To create the arrangement, they use living, dried, or artificial plant material and a variety of tools, such as foam, trimmers, wire, and floral tape. Floral design jobs are less competitive and require less education than other design jobs, but they also pay less well. Salaries begin around $10,000; designers with more than three years experience make around $15,000.

Fur Designer *(ACS)*

Fur designers design garments made of fur for individual customers or the commercial fur apparel industry. Combining their knowledge of fashion and fur, they sketch a design, take customer measurements, draw a pattern and cut canvas to construct a mock garment. After checking the fit and making alterations, they direct those who sew the fur and then examine the finished product. Fur designers may also redesign fur garments and estimate the costs involved in making new or restyled fur fashions.

Furniture Designer *(AES)*

Furniture designers work for furniture manufacturers, designing furniture and fixtures (fixtures are furniture that doesn't move, such as display cases). After studying the market, brainstorming ideas, and considering production feasibility, they sketch an article of furniture. If approved, they draw a to-scale original, prepare an itemized list of production requirements, help prepare blueprints, and specify the kinds of material to be used in building the article. They may build models or direct others to build models. The salaries of furniture designers range from $12,000 to over $50,000, with a median salary in 1990 of $26,000.

Graphic Designer *(AER)*

Graphic designers design the pages of publications and the visual part of advertising. They choose design elements—such as illustrations or photographs and type style and size—and arrange them pleasingly on the page. They prepare sample layouts, instruct people who prepare the final layout, and review it to see if changes need to be made. Graphic designers may design annual reports or company logos. Graphic designers for TV commercials will draw a story board, which is a series of cartoon scenes used to guide the visual part of producing a commercial.

Graphic designers are employed by newspapers, book and magazine publishers, TV and film studios, retail stores, design studios, advertising agencies, public relations firms, greeting card companies, and corporate advertising departments. In 1992, the average salary for graphic designers was $20,800. Salaries range from $31,000 to $48,500 in corporate design departments; $51,500 to $103,000 in advertising agencies; and $36,000 to $62,000 in design studios.

Industrial Designer *(AES)*

Industrial designers design manufactured products such as vehicles, toys, appliances, and other equipment. They research products, generate and evaluate design ideas based on practical and esthetic considerations, and then develop designs that are functional, visually appealing, and competitive. They sketch and present their designs, modifying them after discussion. Industrial designers are employed by consulting firms and large manufacturing companies. In 1992, salaries ranged from $27,000 to $45,000, depending on experience; industrial designers with executive responsibilities could make as much as $75,000.

Interior Designer *(ASE)*

Interior designers plan, design, and furnish interior space in many different kinds of buildings, both public and private. Bringing together their knowledge of client taste and budget with interior design principles, they design space that is functional and esthetically pleasing. They draw and illustrate their plans for the client, including specifications for furnishings and lighting, advise clients about color and layout, and select furnishings, floor coverings, curtains, and accessories.

Interior designers are employed by architectural or interior design firms, department stores and home furnishings stores, corporations, furniture and textile manufacturers, design magazines, and hotel, restaurant, and theater chains. Many are self-employed. Average salaries in 1993 were $25,000 for junior designers, $38,000 for senior designers, and $50,500 for project managers.

≋

173

Landscape Architect *(AIR)*

Landscape architects design parks; golf courses; commercial, industrial, and residential sites; and other land development projects. They work with engineers and architects to serve organizations like municipalities or real estate development firms. To begin, they gather and analyze information from a site, such as soil condition, water drainage, sun exposure, established vegetation, and already existing facilities. Then they prepare plans for the site that integrate new facilities and foliage. Once approved, they draw up detailed plans, methods of construction, and lists of materials.

Landscape architects are employed by architectural firms and firms that provide landscape architecture services. Some work for the federal government, and some are self-employed. The median salary for landscape architects in 1992 was $41,900.

Memorial Designer *(AER)*

Memorial designers design the stonework used in cemeteries, including monuments and statues. After consulting with clients to learn their preferences, they design a memorial and carve their design into a plaster model. The model and specifications are then passed on to a stone carver. Memorial designers may also plan family plots and build models of cemeteries. Memorial designers are employed by memorial studios, monument companies, and the larger quarries and fabricators of granite.

Package Designer *(AEI)*

Package designers design containers for products like food and cosmetics and drugs. After learning about the market and practical requirements for packaging, they create designs that will attract customers, be relatively simple to produce, convenient to store and handle, and easy to identify. Usually they build models using whatever materials will be used in the packaging, making changes in design as necessary. Package designers are employed by package design firms, graphic design studios that specialize in packaging, advertising agencies, and corporations.

Safety-Clothing-and-Equipment Developer *(AER)*

Safety-clothing-and-equipment developers design clothing and equipment to protect workers in hazardous conditions. After researching hazardous conditions (such as fire or toxic fumes) by consulting with the people involved, they design suits and helmets that might include protective devices such as mechanical breathing apparatus or communication systems. To make the first pattern of a suit or component part, they draft full-scale pattern parts on paper. Then they tell employees how to cut and construct material to make a sample item.

Set Decorator *(AES)*

Set decorators decorate sets for movies and TV shows. They read the scripts and choose decorations such as lamps, rugs, window treatments, and furniture. They direct assistants who place decorations on the set, and then make sure that the dressed set will not interfere with the movements of the cast or the vision of the camera crew. Set decorators find work through film and TV art directors.

Set Designer, Motion Picture *(AIE)*

Set designers design sets for movies. After consulting the art director, they complete the set design, prepare scale construction drawings, and adapt as needed. Miniature set designers design miniature sets that are used as background and for special effects. Set designers find work through art directors or production designers.

Set Designer, Theater *(AES)*

Set designers design sets for theater companies. They learn from the director the requirements for the set and then research the appropriate style for the work to be performed. Keeping budget and scene changes in mind, they draw a design, indicating floor plans, scenery, borders, and props, and then direct the building of the set. They may also build models to scale and design the lighting of the set.

Image Makers

Bonsai Culturist *(RAE)*

Bonsai culturists grow dwarf trees. After selecting small trees that are suitable for bonsai, they prune roots and branches and add chemicals to the soil to stunt growth. Using cutters and wires, they train tree limbs to create artistic forms. They choose esthetic containers in which to plant their trees and arrange moss and rocks and other decorations around them. Bonsai culturists are employed by bonsai nurseries, organizations that collect or exhibit bonsai, and landscape designers who showcase bonsai gardens.

Cartoonist *(AES)*

Cartoonists draw cartoons for print media. After developing their ideas, they sketch a cartoon, get feedback, and make changes. Some cartoonists write their own captions, using talents with humor or criticism. Cartoonists may specialize in sports or editorial cartoons, or comic strips. Cartoonists are hired by newspapers, magazines, news services, and advertising agencies.

Cartoonist, Motion Pictures *(AES)*

Cartoonists for film and TV draw a series of sequential cartoons for animation. They may specialize in characters, backgrounds, or special effects. Cartoonists are employed by animation houses and TV and motion picture studios.

Fashion Artist *(AEI)*

Fashion artists draw illustrations of clothing and accessories for advertisements. They position the item to accentuate its desirable features and then draw or paint it, often including figures and other background. They may also draw lettering. Fashion artists are employed by department stores, mail order catalogs, newspapers, magazines, and fashion advertising agencies.

Illustrator *(AER)*

Illustrators paint or draw pictures to illustrate words in such diverse products as books, magazines, greeting cards, calendars, stationery, and wrapping paper. Observing models or photographs and drawing upon their visual memory or imagination, they draw illustrations, seek feedback, and make changes. They may also do layout, choose type, and draw lettering. Some illustrators specialize in title art and paint or draw the lettering used in titles and commercial logos.

Illustrators are employed by book, magazine, and greeting card publishers; film, video, and paper products producers; and advertising agencies. Most visual artists are self-employed and their income varies widely. Visual artists employed full time earned a median salary of $23,000 in 1992; the middle 50 percent fell in the $17,600 to $30,800 range.

Illustrator, Medical and Scientific *(AIE)*

Medical and scientific illustrators create drawings, diagrams, and three-dimensional models of subjects including pathology, medical procedures, parts of the body, and plant and animal tissue. Their illustrations are done in a variety of media, including pen and ink, watercolor, plastics, and plaster. Their illustrations are used in teaching, research, publications, exhibits, and consultation. Histological illustrators specialize in drawing plant and animal tissue.

Medical and scientific illustrators are employed by medical centers, teaching institutions, and publishers of medical and scientific information, including journals and textbooks. Many are self-employed and may freelance to doctors and lawyers who need exhibits for court cases.

Illustrator, Set *(AES)*

Set illustrators create the backdrop for movies and TV programs. They read the script, do background research, consult with the art director while developing their plans, and then illustrate the background against which movies and TV shows are shot. Set illustrators find work through art directors.

Make-Up Artist *(AER)*

Makeup artists apply makeup to stage and film performers so that their appearance, including facial features, skin texture, and body shape, is appropriate for their roles. In order to create an image of the character, they study sketches and photographs and plaster models in period files. They confer with performers and managers to learn production requirements and then order cosmetics and supplies, such as wigs or beards. They also design and apply prostheses. Salaries for makeup artists range from $12,500 to more than $65,000 a year. Makeup artists are hired by costume designers, theater groups, and makeup companies. They may freelance their services to models, photographers, beauty salons, department stores, advertising agencies, and TV or film production companies.

≈≈≈
177

Painter *(ASI)*

Painters paint original compositions such as landscapes, still lifes, and portraits. Painters are usually self-employed, and sell their work to individual art collectors and to stores, museums, and art galleries. They may also do murals and other large decorative work for businesses and local community groups, as well as air-brush work on vehicles, T-shirts, and other media.

Pewterer *(ARS)*

Pewterers design new merchandise for manufacturers of pewter products. Using their knowledge of metallurgy and mold-making, they fabricate models of new casting molds, mix and heat alloy, fill casting molds, and finish the product using a variety of tools such as lathes and blowtorches. To facilitate the finishing process, they adapt tools and fabricate lathe accessories as needed. Once production is underway, they analyze its efficiency.

Police Artist *(ASC)*

Police artists work for law enforcement agencies, sketching crime scenes and likenesses of criminal suspects. In order to draw a suspected criminal, they question victims and witnesses about the suspect's body type, facial features, and other identifying characteristics and then sketch a series of simple line drawings that fit the descriptions. Once their informants choose a drawing most like the suspect, police artists ask for additional information and then draw a picture that more closely resembles the suspect. They may work from photographs or sketch on site to prepare schematic drawings of the scene of the crime.

Printmaker *(AES)*

Printmakers conceive and develop printed images for designs that they etch or engrave or carve into material such as wood or stone or metal. They choose a printmaking method, render the drawing, ink the surface, and transfer the image to paper or other textured surface. Some printmakers use computer-driven data to create inkjet prints. After initial proofs have been examined and corrected, they print, approve, and sign the final proof. Printmakers are employed by printmaking studios and sell their work to collectors and art galleries and museums.

Quick Sketch Artist *(ASE)*

Quick sketch artists draw likenesses of their customers. After posing their customers to highlight appealing features, they use pencil, charcoal, or pastels to draw a quick picture. Some artists work from photographs. Caricaturists draw only exaggerated likenesses. Quick sketch artists are self-employed, usually working in tourist spots or arts festivals.

Sculptor *(AER)*

Sculptors create three-dimensional works of art from materials such as stone, concrete, wood, or metal, using tools such as chisels, mallets, abrasives, and soldering irons. They may carve their forms from a block of marble, model wax forms and cast them in bronze, model clay forms and fire them in kilns, and arrange and fasten together various man-made and natural materials. Sculptors may get public commissions. They sell their work to individual collectors and those who request private portraits as well as to art galleries, stores, and museums.

Silhouette Artist *(AES)*

Silhouette artists draw and cut freehand silhouettes of their customers. They pose their customer, sometimes using lights to cast a shadow. After cutting the silhouette, they place it on contrasting paper and may also mount it. Silhouette artists are self-employed, working in department stores and arts festivals.

Stained-Glass Artist *(ASE)*

Stained-glass artists create original designs for art objects and windows made of stained glass. They consult with clients to learn the kind of treatment desired, study the surrounding architecture and window shape, and integrate practical requirements with a knowledge of glass cutting and symbolic imagery. After drawing the design and estimating cost for the client, they make a full size working pattern and select and cut glass according to the pattern. They may assemble the pieces, secure them in place, paint or stain the glass and fire it to stabilize the colors, and may install the finished window. Stained-glass artists freelance and are hired by stained-glass studios, churches, and businesses.

Photographers

Camera Operator *(AES)*

Camera operators take photographs using film, TV broadcasting, or video cameras and equipment. They may set up and operate equipment such as dollies, cranes, and power zooms. During filming they monitor and solve problems related to exposure, movement, and distance. They may maintain their equipment and perform minor repairs. Some camera operators specialize in a particular field, such as news, commercials, cartoons, or special effects. Camera operators specializing in film are also called motion picture photographers.

Camera operators are employed by TV stations or film studios. Other employers include independent production firms, advertising agencies, corporate media centers, the government, and educational institutions. Salaries for videographers ranged from less than $10,000 to more than $37,000 in 1991.

Director of Photography *(AES)*

Directors of photography, also known as cinematographers, plan and direct the filming of motion pictures. After learning about cinematic effects desired from the director, they look over the set or location and determine the lighting and photographic equipment needed. They choose camera angles and depth of focus and so on; select appropriate equipment; and then instruct the camera crew in setting up cameras at the proper distance. During filming they observe lighting, make adjustments, and signal the beginning and end of filming. After filming they review the film to see if further adjustments need to be made. Some directors of photography specialize in filming special effects. They are employed by film producers and directors.

Photographer, Still *(ARS)*

Still photographers use still cameras and color or black-and-white film to photograph a variety of subjects. They choose appropriate equipment, plan a composition, position the camera and subject, measure light and distance or create their own light, adjust lens aperture and shutter speed, and take pictures. Some photographers develop their own pictures and may touch up negatives or prints. Photographers may specialize in areas such as portraits, weddings, fashion, nature, or architecture.

Portrait studios and commercial photography studios employ photographers, as do newspapers, magazines, advertising agencies, and the government. Almost half of U.S. photographers are self-employed. They may contract work to the above employers, run a small portrait photography business, or sell photos to stock photo services. Median salary for full-time photographers in 1992 was 21,200, with a range from less than $12,300 to more than $49,200.

Photojournalist *(AEC)*

Photojournalists photograph newsworthy subjects with still cameras. They travel to an assigned location to take pictures, later developing their film and turning their photos or negatives over to an editor. Photojournalists are employed by print media including newspapers, magazines, and other journals. In 1990, photojournalists who were employed by newspapers had a average starting minimum wage of $425 a week and an average starting salary of $650 a week.

Performers

Laserist *(ASI)*

Laserists create optical shows to entertain audiences, projecting laser designs that are accompanied by music. They also maintain optical and sound equipment, testing and repairing equipment as necessary. Laserists work at planetariums and amusement parks and for producers of packaged laser shows. They may also freelance.

Magician *(AES)*

Magicians perform sleight-of-hand tricks using props such as rabbits, scarves, and cards to create illusions that mystify and entertain. Corporations sometimes hire magicians to deliver a product message at trade shows, sales meetings, and hospitality suites. Magicians also find work through entertainment agencies and event-planning services and appear at nightclubs, birthday parties, and banquets.

Musician, Instrumental *(ASI)*

Instrumental musicians perform as soloists or as members of a band or orchestra or other musical group. In addition to playing music they may also compose, improvise, or transpose. Accompanists are instrumental musicians who accompany other musicians.

Instrumental musicians are hired by professional orchestras and symphonies; chamber music groups; recording companies; producers of ballet, musicals, opera, films, and TV shows or commercials; churches and synagogues; clubs, cruise ships, and restaurants; and the planners of weddings and other social or cultural events. Recording musicians may earn a minimum of $245 for a three-hour session. Church musician salaries range from $7,000 to $27,500 per year.

Puppeteer *(AEI)*

Puppeteers create puppet shows from beginning to end: they come up with an idea for a show, write an original script or adaptation of a story, design and construct puppets for each role, and then animate them during performance, giving them a voice through talking or singing or operating audio equipment. Puppeteers most commonly make hand, string, shadow, or rod puppets; some use animatronic devices. Puppeteers work for puppet companies, children's theaters and children's museums, TV stations, and amusement parks. Self-employed puppeteers may entertain at school assemblies, company picnics, and birthday parties, also finding work through entertainment agencies and event-planning services.

Electronic Designers

Computer Artist *(ASE)*

Computer artists use computers to format printed information such as newsletters, brochures, and magazines. They choose such design elements as color and type size and style. Computer artists are hired by publishing companies, desktop publishers, advertising agencies, and in-house advertising departments.

Film or Videotape Editor *(AES)*

Film editors use film splicers to edit film; videotape editors use editing equipment to edit videotape and soundtracks. After selecting and cutting segments based on their visual appeal as well as their educational or enter-tainment value, editors reassemble segments to achieve continuity and dramatic effect. Some editors specialize in areas such as news, music, ani-mation, sound effects, and electronic graphics. Film and videotape editors work for producers of motion pictures, motion picture studios, TV sta-tions, cable companies, independent production companies, production and postproduction facilities, corporate television centers, media centers, and advertising agencies.

Media Production Specialist *(AES)*

Media production specialists use audiovisual technology to produce edu-cational materials. When planning video productions, they coordinate the work of writers, designers, and actors. They arrange for settings and props before directing the production. Some set up and run cameras and other media equipment. Media production specialists are employed by corpo-rations, nonprofits, educational institutions, video and film production companies, advertising agencies, TV stations and networks, and the gov-ernment. In 1991, their salaries ranged from less than $20,000 to over $37,000.

Program Director, Cable Television *(EAS)*

Cable TV program directors work at cable TV stations, operating video-tape equipment and coordinating the work of employees who select and produce cable TV programs. They hire workers and instruct them in maintenance and operation of TV equipment. They write a script and rehearse it with entertainers, coordinating the script with sound, music, and visuals to produce a show. When filming and editing a program, they operate cameras, sound mixers, videotape decks, and other equipment. Cable TV program directors also prepare a budget and perform public relations functions, such as writing press releases.

Programmer-Analyst *(IAC)*

Programmer-analysts fill the role of both computer programmer and sys-tems analyst, using their knowledge of programming techniques and computer systems to develop computer programs. They may also design the computer screen display, document their work, and write a user's manual. Programmer-analysts are employed by most industries, especially data-processing service organizations. Included among these are government agencies, insurance companies, educational and financial institutions, manufacturers of computer/electronic equipment or computing/accounting machines, and software development companies that create software for everything from desktop publishing to computer games. In 1992, median salaries for full-time programmers were $35,600; median salaries for full-time systems analysts were $42,100.

Television Technician *(ASI)*

Television technicians perform a variety of duties both in and outside the TV studio. Their duties include operating studio cameras or portable cameras; operating video consoles to transmit TV scenes; producing films or videotapes for educational and training purposes; and setting up and operating other equipment used for TV broadcasting, such as lights, microphones, and recording systems. TV technicians also maintain their equipment and perform minor repairs.

Finishers

Artist, Suspect

Working from information provided by the victim of (or a witness to) a crime, suspect artists assemble images of possible suspects, using a kit or, increasingly, a computer program, modifying them until the interviewee is satisfied that the image resembles the suspect. They also search police records for possible matches.

Body-Make-Up Artist *(AER)*

Body-make-up artists apply makeup to the bodies of performers so that their bodies will match their faces in tone and texture. After preparing grease paint or liquid makeup of the desired shade, they use fingers or sponge to apply it to exposed areas of the performer's body. Body-make-up artists are hired by costume designers, theater groups, make-up companies, individual entertainers, and producers of entertainment.

Copyist *(AES)*

Apparel manufacturing firms hire copyists to gather information on fashion trends and sketch detailed examples of clothing made by competitors. Copyists attend fashion shows, review fashion magazines, read trade publications and talk to people in the garment industry to learn about new trends, consumer preferences, and price ranges.

Crafter, Jewelry *(ARE)*

Crafters follow drawings or instructions to make sample jewelry for accessories manufacturing firms. Using metal cutting and shaping tools, they cut and shape metal, softening metal findings with a gas torch and soldering pieces together according to jewelry design. They smooth and polish rough surfaces and attach stones and other decorative trimmings.

Decorator, Mannequin *(RAE)*

Mannequin decorators work for mannequin manufacturers, using hand brushes and airbrushes to paint faces on mannequins. They mix paint, then follow a model and paint lifelike facial features on a mannequin head. They also measure, cut, and attach eyelashes. Then they spray a protective coating on the finished head.

Engrosser *(ARE)*

Engrossers are also known as calligraphers. Using pen and ink, they letter diplomas, testimonials, citations, and other formal documents. Illuminators are a kind of engrosser that designs and draws initial letters, scrollwork, and borders for books and posters. Calligraphers are employed by engrossing firms and greeting card companies. Engrossers may freelance to individuals and to a variety of organizations such as hospitals, schools, advertising agencies, public relations firms, and corporations.

Exhibit Artist *(ASI)*

Exhibit artists work for museums and zoos and similar establishments, producing artwork for permanent or temporary exhibits. After consulting professional staff about the purpose of the exhibit and the type of artwork desired, they make scale drawings that indicate the size and position of artwork within the exhibit. Following the designer's layout, they paint a background on burlap, canvas, or wood and prepare titles and legends for the exhibit, painting or stenciling or mounting letters cut from plastic or plywood. They photograph appropriate objects, developing negatives and modifying prints to conform to the exhibit's design. They also fashion accessories, such as trees, relief maps, and human figures.

Instructor, Painting *(AES)*
Painting instructors work for retailers, indirectly promoting sales by teaching ornamental painting. They select plaques and fabrics and other materials for customers, demonstrate painting techniques, and give advice on purchases.

Milliner *(AES)*
Milliners make hats for retail stores, cutting material to follow an original pattern or copying the design of an existing hat. Using hat forms and a steam iron, they mold, drape, and block material and then sew it together, trimming it with flowers, veils, ribbons, and other decorations. Milliners also alter hats for customers.

Optical-Effects Camera Operator *(ARS)*
Optical-effects camera operators set up and operate cameras and optical printers to produce fades, dissolves, superimpositions, and other optical effects on film. After analyzing specifications, they load the camera of an optical-effects printer, adjust camera position and settings, select filters for appropriate light and intensity, and film specified optical effects. Optical-effects camera operators also set up and operate animation cameras, matte cameras, and subtitle cameras. They are employed in postproduction facilities and may also find work through directors of photography.

Optical-Effects Layout Person *(ASC)*
Optical-effects layout people locate and mark frames of motion picture film to identify segments that will be processed for optical effects. Using a splicing device, they splice strips of leader material and assemble film segments as specified. They also clean and repair film. Optical-effects layout people are employed by film labs and postproduction facilities.

Painter, Hand *(ARE)*
Hand painters work for manufacturers in any industry, decorating objects such as pottery, glassware, and china. They may sketch a design first or paint freehand. After grinding colors, they mix them with oils and apply them with hand brushes.

Pewter Finisher *(RAS)*

Pewter finishers work for manufacturers of pewter products, shaping, joining, engraving, and polishing pewter items after they have been cast. Using a lathe, they pare inner and outer surfaces, remove rough edges, and shape the piece to specifications. Pewter finishers engrave decorative lines and polish the surface and, using solder and blowtorch, join parts together.

Sound-Effects Technician *(RAE)*

Sound-effects technicians work for radio and television studios, producing artificial sounds in synchrony with the broadcast. Using previously recorded sounds, they transmit them at the same time the production is presented, in order to give the audience the impression that the action is accompanied by sound.

Stone Carver *(RAE)*

Stone carvers carve designs and figures in full and bas-relief on stone. Following a designer's sketch, blueprint, or model, they transfer the dimensions of the design onto the stone's surface. Using chisels and pneumatic tools, they rough out the design and then further shape, trim, and smooth the stone, periodically stopping to compare and measure the dimensions of their work with that of the model. Stone carvers are employed by memorial studios, monument companies, the larger quarries and fabricators of granite, and contractors who build stone edifices.

Tattoo Artist *(AEC)*

Tattoo artists apply tattoos to the skin of customers. After shaving and washing the area that will receive the tattoo, they trace a stencil or draw an outline of the design onto the skin, then apply the ink using an electric tattoo gun. Between customers they sterilize needles, mix pigments, repair tools, and create original designs. Tattoo artists work in tattoo shops or salons. Many are self-employed.

Wallcovering Texturer *(ASR)*

Wallcovering texturers work for wallpaper manufacturers, dripping or sponging paint in a specified pattern to create texture. Consulting the product card and paint sample book, they apply the specified color in the manner and pattern prescribed.

Model Builders

Concrete Sculptor *(RAI)*

Concrete sculptors construct models and molds for manufacturers of concrete garden furniture and statuary. They build a metal framework to support their model, model clay according to drawings or pictures, brush layers of rubber paint onto their clay model to form a cast, and then cover the cast with a shield of fiberglass. Once the fiberglass has hardened, they cut the layers of rubber and fiberglass into sections, remove and reassemble them, and fill them with concrete.

Exhibit Builder *(ARS)*

Exhibit builders work for museums, constructing exhibit structures and installing electric wiring and other fixtures in the framework. They study sketches to determine materials needed and discuss possible problems with museum personnel. Using hand tools and power tools, they construct the framework and its components, such as shelves or shadowboxes, and finish the structure by applying paint or textured surfaces, affixing murals or photographs, and mounting legends or graphics. Once the exhibit is assembled and installed, they test mechanical and electrical components to make sure they work.

Glass Blower, Laboratory Apparatus *(RAE)*

Laboratory apparatus glass blowers blow and shape glass for medical and laboratory purposes. Knowing the effects of heat and chemicals, they develop specifications for custom glass products such as flasks, test tubes, and chambers. They heat glass tubing and blow, shape, and join it into the required dimensions, later examining and measuring their products to make sure they conform to specifications. Laboratory apparatus glass blowers are employed by universities, research labs, and glass manufacturers.

Modeler, Brick and Tile *(ARI)*

Modelers mold original designs, such as fountains and waterspouts, in decorative tile. They cut and scrape and finish plaster of paris to sculpture a model, sometimes constructing a wooden mold to cast clay models. Modelers work on commission to individuals or organizations. Some are employed by manufacturers of brick and tile products.

Model Maker, Pottery and Porcelain *(RAE)*

Model makers work for manufacturers of pottery and porcelain, constructing models of pieces that will be used for casting molds. Working with plaster and/or clay, they shape it with their hands or shave it with steel cutting tools as it revolves on the spinning table.

Model Maker *(ARI)*

Model makers work for industries such as ship or boat builders or automobile manufacturers, building models to scale. Using materials such as wood, fiberglass, or metal, they construct a scale model of the object to be manufactured.

188

Miniature-Set Constructor *(ARE)*

Miniature-set constructors build miniature models of motion picture sets for filming backgrounds, titles, and special effects. They cut and fit building materials with hand tools to form three-dimensional set pieces and they form landscapes and foliage. They trim and paint the completed set. Miniature-set constructors are employed by production designers and post-production facilities. They may find work through art directors.

Stage Technician *(ARS)*

Stage technicians erect stages and install rigging, lighting, scenery, and sound equipment. They consult the stage manager and stage blueprints, and assemble sets, props, and scenery. Using electrician's tools and their knowledge of electrical codes, they position lighting and sound equipment and connect electrical wiring. During rehearsal and performance, they pull cables to raise and lower curtains and scenery, and operate lighting and sound equipment. Stage technicians are employed by theaters and production companies. Some work in arenas, stadiums, and amusement parks.

Food Preparers

Cake Decorator *(ARE)*

Cake decorators use an icing bag or paper cone to decorate pastries and cakes. After trimming and cutting the cake to a desired shape, they spread frosting, tint icing, and squeeze it out of a bag while designing decorations. Cake decorators work in retail bakeries and retail eating places, grocery stores, and institutional kitchens.

Chef de Froid *(RAE)*

A chef de froid designs decorations for food and creates artistic arrangements of food for formal buffets. They prepare and decorate foods like hors d'oeuvres, casseroles, and relishes; mold butter; sculpt ice; carve meat; and arrange fruits and vegetables. Chefs de froid usually work in formal restaurants, including those in hotels and country clubs and on cruise ships. Other employers are cooking schools and caterers for movie companies and special events.

Cook, Pastry *(RAS)*

Pastry cooks prepare cakes, cookies, custards, pies, puddings, and other desserts, which they may decorate with toppings, icings, and ornaments. Pastry cooks work in restaurants, hotels, government and factory cafeterias, grocery stores, bakery shops, and the kitchens of nursing homes, hospitals, and educational institutions.

Decorator, Dairy Products *(AES)*

Dairy products decorators mold and decorate ice cream confections. Using spatulas, stencils, spray guns, and whipped cream dispensers, they create designs and figures. Dairy products decorators are employed by ice cream and frozen yogurt establishments, large hotels, cruise ships, restaurants serving gourmet desserts, and caterers serving the media.

Ice Cream Chef *(RAS)*

Ice cream chefs make ice cream, sherbets, and other frozen desserts with sauces and syrups, then decorate them. Ice cream chefs work in restaurants, ice cream parlors, and ice cream production companies.

Restorers

Musical Instrument Repairer *(RAS/E)*

Musical instrument repairers adjust and repair musical instruments such as violins, guitars, accordions, and clarinets. After inspecting and playing the instrument to pinpoint problems, they disassemble it, repair or replace parts, and reassemble it. They may tune the instrument and play it to be sure it is properly repaired. Musical instrument repairers work in music stores and repair shops. Some are self-employed.

Paintings Conservator *(ASR)*

Paintings conservators preserve and restore paintings that are faded or damaged. Using photographs or magnifying devices, they examine a painting and test its surface to select appropriate cleaning solvents. After removing the painting from the frame, they clean the surface and apply beeswax and paint where needed, blending their work to maintain the style of the original. They may laminate parts of a painting together or apply a preservative to its surface. In addition to preservation, they research the original work to determine the extent of loss and may plan the care of a entire collection. Paintings conservators are hired by museums, institutions with painting collections, regional conservation centers, historical sites and houses, and private collectors. Some are self-employed.

Restorer, Ceramic *(ASI)*

Ceramic restorers work for museums cleaning, preserving, and restoring ceramic ware. They recommend preservation measures, such as light or heat control, to prevent damage or deterioration, as well as repairing broken wares to reproduce their original appearance. Ceramic restorers also construct replicas of ceramic ware, basing their design on existing remnants and their knowledge of ceramic history.

Restorer, Paper-and-Prints *(AIS)*

Paper-and-prints restorers work for libraries and museums, cleaning, preserving, restoring, and repairing paper objects of historic and artistic importance. First they examine the book, document, map, print, or photograph to identify the problem and plan the safest and most effective treatment. For example, they may clean paper by dry cleaning, wet cleaning, or applying solvent to stains; they may preserve paper by laminating or spraying it or immersing it in a deacidification bath; they may restore paper by bleaching it or strengthening it with gelatin; they may repair paper by patching worm holes or retouching pictures to reproduce the effects of the original artist.

Trail 4: Ideas & People & Things

Teachers

Teacher, Art *(ASE)*

Art teachers teach skills such as painting, designing, or sculpturing and may specialize in teaching a particular field such as art history, graphic design, or illustration. After preparing lesson plans and selecting textbooks and supplies, they demonstrate artistic techniques, observe and evaluate their students' work, and provide feedback. Art teachers may also arrange field trips, organize student contests, or plan art exhibits. Art teachers are employed by educational institutions, correctional facilities, and community agencies. They also teach private lessons to individuals and offer workshops through guilds and other organizations. The average salary for art teachers in public schools is $36,500.

~~~
191

Teacher, Music *(AES)*

Music teachers teach instrumental music and voice to both individuals and groups, including instruction in such subjects as music appreciation, music theory, and composition. They evaluate the personality and aptitude of an individual student when choosing a beginning instrument and prepare and teach lessons that include demonstration of musical skills and critiques of performance. Music teachers conduct rehearsals, coach individuals, and lead groups in public performance. They may also meet with parents, arrange field trips, and store musical instruments and supplies. Music teachers are employed by educational institutions, including schools, universities, and conservatories. Some work for theaters. Many are self-employed. Public school teachers earn an average salary of $36,500.

Supervisors

Art Director *(AES)*

Art directors formulate persuasive concepts to be presented by magazines, posters, TV, and other media, and supervise workers who prepare art layouts. After reviewing the material to be presented and learning the client's objectives and constraints, they formulate a basic layout design concept and select illustrations. They may prepare art design layouts themselves or assign staff members to prepare layouts. Then they review, approve, and present final layouts to the client. Art directors work in advertising agencies, in-house advertising departments, and publishing companies.

Inspector, Screen Printing *(ASR)*

Screen printing inspectors inspect stencils, silk screens, and printed products. They examine customer orders and materials to evaluate their suitability for silk-screen printing, return unsatisfactory stencils to the cutter, and examine a sample of screen printing to verify that color and print conform to the customer's request. Later they inspect the final product. Screen printing inspectors are employed by screen printing companies and manufacturers of printed products, including banners, novelties, T-shirts, and sweatshirts.

Manager, Display *(AES)*

Display managers develop interior advertising displays and supervise workers who lay out and assemble them. After consulting with advertising and sales people to learn when and where particular merchandise is to be displayed, they develop a layout that integrates theme, color, light, and props. Then they order necessary materials and oversee construction. Display managers work for retail establishments and display houses that produce displays for showrooms, special events, and trade shows.

Pastry Chef *(ASE/ARE)*

Pastry chefs are considered supervisors, as they mainly coordinate the activities of the workers who actually prepare desserts, confections, and pastries, although some may create these items themselves. They plan dessert menus, order supplies, and supervise production. The different Holland codes apply to different work locales: chefs employed in hotels, restaurants, retail bakeries and cafeterias are coded ASE; those employed by passenger or cruise ships, ARE.

Supervisor, Suspect Artist *(ASE)*

Suspect artist supervisors work for law enforcement agencies in very large cities, coordinating the activities of workers who form composite images of criminal suspects. Like the artists they train and supervise, they also arrange and enhance sets of facial features to form composite images.

Supervisor, Scenic Arts *(AES)*

Scenic arts supervisors create layouts of scenery and backdrops and supervise artists who paint them. After consulting with the art director they prepare sketches, estimate the amount of paint and the number of workers needed, and the cost of supplies before preparing a budget. Scenic arts supervisors work in film and TV sound stages; some find work through art directors.

193

Entertainers

Acrobat *(AER)*

Acrobats entertain an audience by performing spectacular feats that involve balancing, juggling, and/or tumbling. Performing alone or with others, they may adapt stock routines or create original acts. Acrobats are employed by circuses and may occasionally find work with theater companies or through event-planning services or entertainment agencies.

Amusement Park Entertainer *(AES)*

Amusement park entertainers entertain their audience by performing a specialty act such fire eating, snake charming, sword swallowing, organ grinding, or "reading" character from a person's expression or head shape. Amusement park entertainers find work in amusement parks, nightclubs, and live variety shows.

Double *(AER)*

Doubles portray stars of motion pictures or TV movies. Dressing in the same costume as the star, they imitate the performer's gestures and mannerisms, either facing away from the camera or at a distance from the camera. Doubles are employed by film and television producers and studios.

Equestrian *(AER)*

Equestrians entertain an audience by riding horses, performing acrobatic stunts or other feats of skill and daring. Bareback riders perform on horses without saddles. Equestrians work at circuses, carnivals, horse shows, and other exhibitions.

Impersonator, Character *(EAS)*

Character impersonators dress up in costumes and impersonate holiday characters, such as Santa Claus or the Easter Bunny, or storybook characters, such as Mickey Mouse or Cinderella. They may talk with parents and children, hand out gifts or samples, ask for donations, pose for pictures, take part in parades, or demonstrate something for sale. Character impersonators may be hired to promote sales at retail stores, conventions, or exhibits, or to amuse children at restaurants, hospitals, or amusement parks.

Psychic Reader *(AEC)*

Psychic readers entertain an audience by using psychic abilities to tell about past or future events. They may gaze into crystal balls, tell fortunes, or read palms, cards, or tea leaves. Psychic readers may work for hot lines or find work through entertainment agencies. Some volunteer their services at police departments; some work at fairs or carnivals. Self-employed psychics develop a private clientele, sometimes selling their services through 900-number lines.

Ring Conductor *(EAS)*

Ring conductors work for circuses, introducing acts in a style requested by the management. Using a schedule of performances, they announce the beginning and ending of individual acts and signal the performers to create smooth transitions between acts. In the event of an accident or other emergency, they address the concerns of the audience.

Singing Messenger *(ASC)*

Singing messengers work for message delivery services, singing and dancing as they deliver messages to specific people. After learning song and dance routines, they take a customer's message, dress up in makeup and costume if necessary, travel to and find the recipient of the message, and perform the routine. They may play a musical instrument during the performance or deliver a gift afterwards.

Wire Walker *(AER)*

Wire walkers are also known as high-wire artists or tightrope walkers. They perform on a high wire or rope or cable, walking or riding bikes or performing stunts—such as headstands or somersaults—that require balance and acrobatic skill. Wire walkers are employed by circuses.

Care-Givers

Child Care Attendant *(SAI)*

Child care attendants help prekindergarten children, organizing and leading activities in preschools and playrooms. They read to children, set up art projects, teach games and songs, and help children develop habits of self-care. They also maintain discipline, serve meals, and monitor rest periods. Child care attendants work in nursery schools, preschools, child daycare centers, and playrooms provided by organizations such as theaters, department stores, hotels, and historic sites. In 1992, early childhood assistants earned a median weekly full-time salary of $220.

≋≋

195

Models

Model *(EAS)*

Models model clothing for customers, buyers, salespeople, and garment designers. Dressing in coats, suits, swimwear, or other garments, they stand, turn, and walk to demonstrate the features of the clothes they wear. Models work in department stores, custom salons, manufacturers' showrooms, fashion shows, and trade shows.

Model, Artists' *(AES)*

Artists' models pose as a subject for painters and sculptors and other visual artists. They may specialize in nude or clothed posing, perhaps providing their own costumes. They are employed by art schools, artists' organizations, and individual artists.

Model, Photographers' *(AES)*

Photographers' models pose for pictures that are used to advertise merchandise. After applying makeup and styling their hair, they pose as instructed by the photographer or strike their own interpretive poses. Some models specialize in just one part of the body, such as legs, or just one category of merchandise, such as fashion. Photographers' models are self-employed, finding work through modeling agencies and occasionally advertising agencies. Some work directly for photographers.

In addition to the *Dictionary of Occupational Titles,* the following references were used in assembling this appendix:

Field, Shelly. *Career Opportunities in Theater and the Performing Arts.* New York, NY: Fact on File, 1992.

Guiley, Rosemary. *Career Opportunities for Writers,* 2nd edition. New York, NY: Facts on File, 1991.

U.S. Department of Labor, Bureau of Labor Statistics. *Occupational Outlook Handbook,* 1994-95 edition. Indianapolis, IN: JIST Works, 1994.

Notes

[1] Holland, John, Fritzche, Barbara, and Powell, Amy. *The Self-Directed Search (SDS) Technical Manual.* Odessa, FL: Psychological Assesment Resources, 1994.

[2] Robinson, Walter. "Art Careers Still Pay Poorly, Surveys Find." *Art in America* no. 78 (February, 1990): page 35.

[3] Wright, John and Dwyer, Edward. *The American Almanac of Jobs and Salaries.* New York: Avon Books, 1990-1991 edition.

[4] Wiener, Yoash, Vardi, Yoav, and Muczyk, Jan. "Antecedents of Employees' Mental Health—The Role of Career and Work Satisfaction." *Journal of Vocational Behavior* no. 19 (1981): pages 50-60.

[5] If you are curious about media anthropology, I recommend that you read my friend Susan's book. Allen, Susan, ed. *Media Anthropology: Informing Global Citizens.* Westport, CN: Gergin & Garvey, 1994.

[6] Wegmann, Robert, Chapman, Robert, and Johnson, Miriam. *Work in the New Economy: Careers and Job Seeking into the 21st Century.* Indianapolis, IN: JIST Works, Inc., 1989.

[7] French, John, et al. *Career Change in Midlife: Stress, Social Support, and Adjustment.* University of Michigan, 1983.

[8] French, John, et al. *The Mechanisms of Job Stress and Strain.* New York: John Wiley, 1982.

[9] I am grateful to Betty Comtois for the original expression of these ideas.

[10] The diagram is in part an adaptation of Harold Lee's treatment on the esthetic attitude in *Perception and Esthetic Value.* Englewood Cliffs, NJ: Prentice-Hall, 1938.

[11] O'Keeffe, Georgia. "About Myself." 1939.

[12] MacKinnon, Donald. *In Search of Human Effectiveness.* Buffalo, NY: Creative Education Foundation, 1978.

[13] Bronowski, Jacob. *The Origins of Knowledge and Imagination.* New Haven, CT: Yale University Press, 1978.

[14] Super, Donald, and Crites, John. *Appraising Vocational Fitness by Means of Psychological Tests.* New York: Harper, 1962.

[15] Craven, E. *The Use of Interest Inventories in Counseling.* Chicago, IL: Science Research Associates, 1961.

[16] Getzels, J., and Csikszentmihalyi, Mihaly. *The Creative Vision: A Longitudinal Study of Problem Finding in Art.* New York, NY: Wiley Interscience, 1976.

[17] Bolles, Richard Nelson. *What Color is Your Parachute?: A Practical Manual for Job-Hunters & Career Changers.* Berkeley, CA: Ten Speed Press, 1995.

[18] Bolles, Richard Nelson. *How to Create a Picture of Your Ideal Job or Next Career.* Berkeley, CA: Ten Speed Press, 1991.

[19] Miller, Arthur, and Mattson, Ralph. *The Truth About You.* Berkeley, CA: Ten Speed Press, 1989.

[20] Toffler, Alvin. *Powershift: Knowledge, Wealth, and Violence at the Edge of the 21st Century.* New York: Bantam Books, 1990.

[21] Reich, Robert. *The Work of Nations: Preparing Ourselves for 21st-Century Capitalism.* New York: Knopf, 1991.

[22] Gottfredson, Gary, and Holland, John. *Dictionary of Holland Occupational Codes.* Second Edition. Odessa, FL: Psychological Assessment Resources, 1989.

[23] U.S. Department of Labor, Employment and Training Administration. *Dictionary of Occupational Titles*, Fourth Edition. Hawthorne, NJ: The Career Press, 1991.

[24] Figler, Howard. *The Complete Job-Search Handbook.* New York, NY: Henry Holt, 1988.

[25] Handy, Charles. *The Age of Unreason.* Boston, MA: Harvard Business School Press, 1990.

[26] Levinson, Jay Conrad. *Earning Money Without a Job.* New York: Henry Holt, 1991.

[27] May, Rollo. *The Courage to Create.* New York: Bantam Books, 1975.

[28] Gendlin, Eugene. "Experimental Psychotherapy. In *Current Psychotherapies*, 2nd Ed., Raymond Corsini, ed. Itasca, IL: F. E. Peacock, Publishers, 1979.

[29] Sher, Barbara with Annie Gottlieb. *Wishcraft: How to Get What You Really Want .* New York: Ballantine Books, 1979.

[30] Sher, Barbara with Barbara Smith. *I Could Do Anything if I Only Knew What it Was.* New York: Delacorte Press, 1994.

[31] Burns, David. *Feeling Good: The New Mood Therapy.* New York: Signet, 1980.

[32] Marlatt, Alan, and Judith Gordon. *Relapse Prevention: Maintenance Strategies in the Treatment of Addictive Behaviors.* New York: The Guilford Press, 1985.

[33] Covey, Stephen. *The Seven Habits of Highly Effective People.* New York: Simon & Schuster, 1989.

[34] Bloom, Benjamin. "The Role of Gifts and Markers in the Development of Talent," in *Exceptional Children* no. 6, vol. 48 (April 1982): pages 510–522.

[35] Geldzahler, Henry. "Career and the Artist," in *The Business of Art,* edited by Lee Evan Caplin. Englewood Cliffs, NJ: Prentice-Hall, 1982.

[36] Hyde, Lewis. *The Gift: Imagination and the Erotic Life of Property.* New York: Vintage Books, 1983.

[37] Fox, Matthew. *Original Blessing: A Primer in Creation Spirituality.* Santa Fe, NM: Bear & Co., 1983.

[38] Schneider, D. *The Psychoanalyst and the Artist.* East Hampton, NY: Alexa Press, 1979.

[39] MacKinnon, Donald. *In Search of Human Effectiveness.* Buffalo, NY: Creative Education Foundation, 1978.

[40] Mullahy, P. *Oedipus: Myth and Complex.* New York: Hermitage Press, 1948.

[41] Bach, Marcus. *The Power of Perfect Liberty.* Englewood Cliffs, NJ: Prentice Hall, 1971.

[42] "The Nation's Leading Arts Planner Says Culture Builds Community," in *The Tarrytown Letter,* no. 27 (May 1983).

[43] Hurt, Harry, III. *For All Mankind.* New York: Atlantic Monthly Press, 1988.